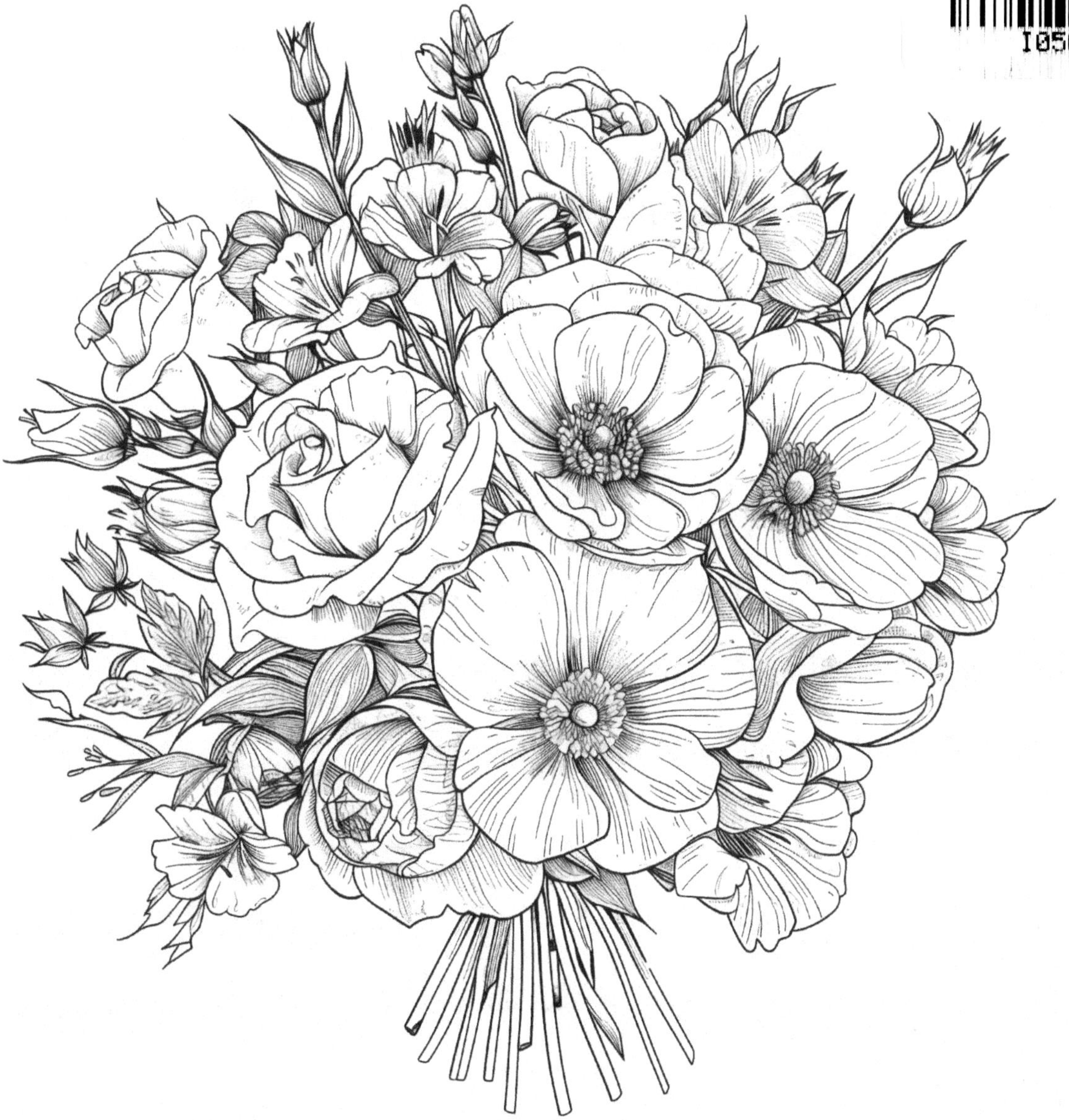

THIS BOOK BELONGS TO :

....

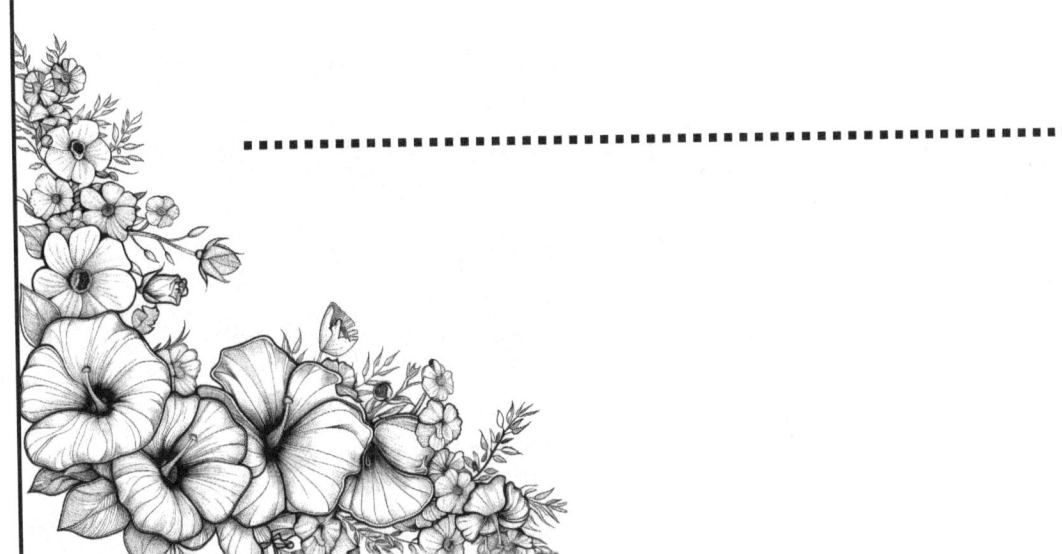

Welcome !

Welcome the renewal and awakening of nature with this colorful journey through the wonders of spring. Through these pages, you will explore a collection of scenes and patterns inspired by spring, carefully crafted to stimulate your creativity and invite you to contemplation.

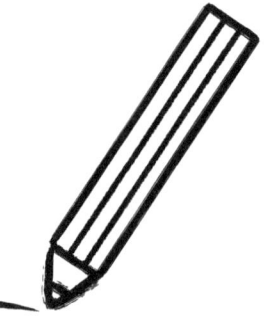

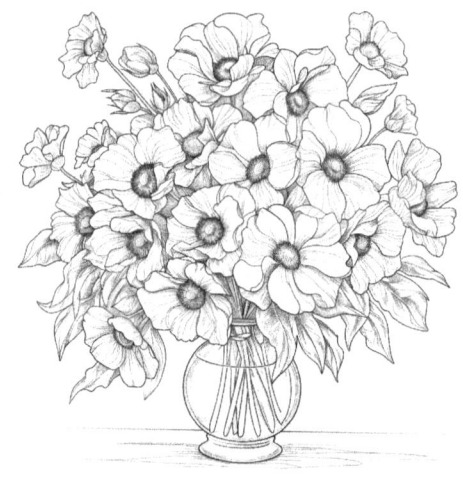

From flowering meadows to awakened forests, each illustration is an invitation to color the world with your vibrant shades.

Immerse yourself in this celebration of renewal, and let each stroke of the pencil guide you towards serenity.

Happy coloring !

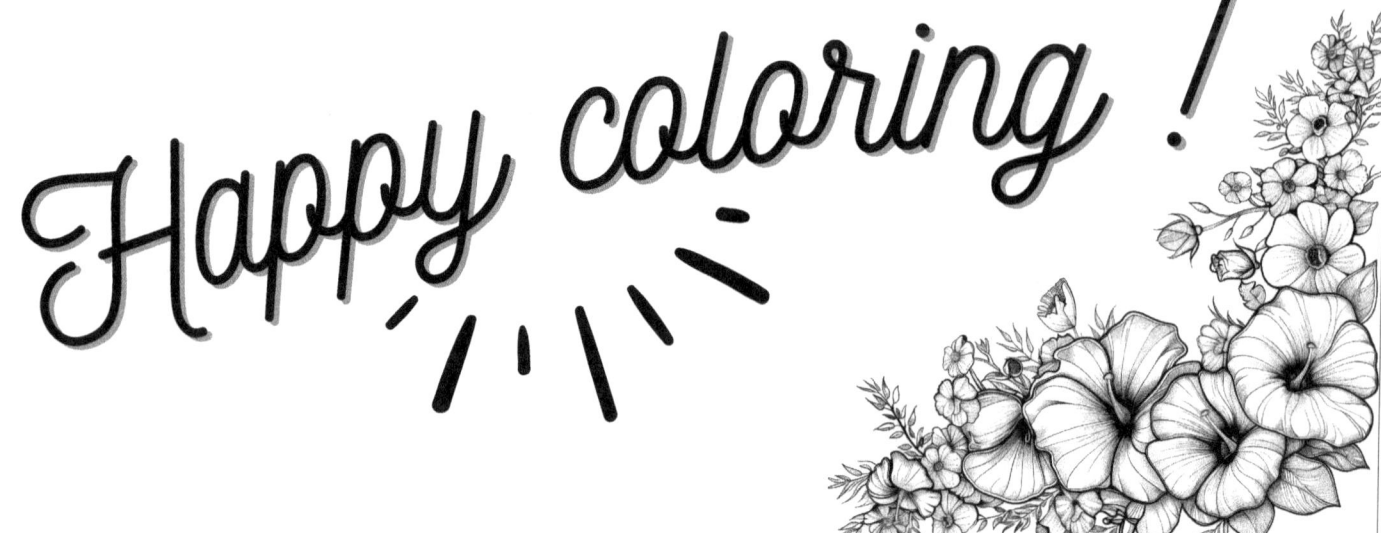

Usage tips

To enrich your coloring experience and preserve the integrity of each drawing, you will find intermediary pages protecting the illustrations from potential smudges or overflows that could alter the following pages, allowing you to create freely.

This notebook features paper that is particularly compatible with a wide range of artistic mediums, including colored pencils, graphite pencils, and pastels. If you prefer alcohol-based markers, I suggest placing a sheet of white paper under the page you are coloring.

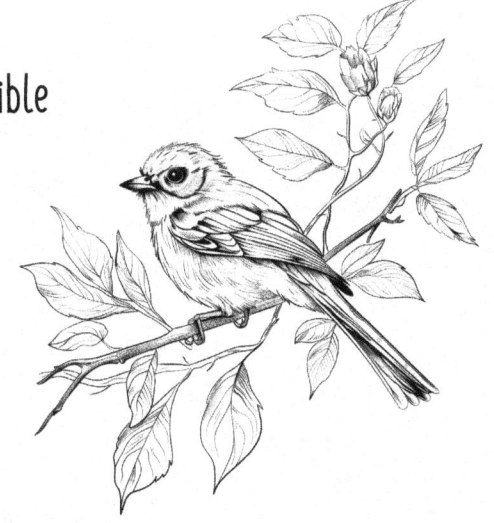

All rights reserved. No part of this publication may be reproduced, distributed, or transmitted in any form or by any means, electronic or mechanical, including photocopying and recording, without the prior written permission of the publisher. Of course, you are encouraged to use short excerpts for your reviews, analyses, or in the context of other non-commercial activities permitted by copyright law. Thank you for your understanding and support in protecting this work.

Want to try

your colors ?

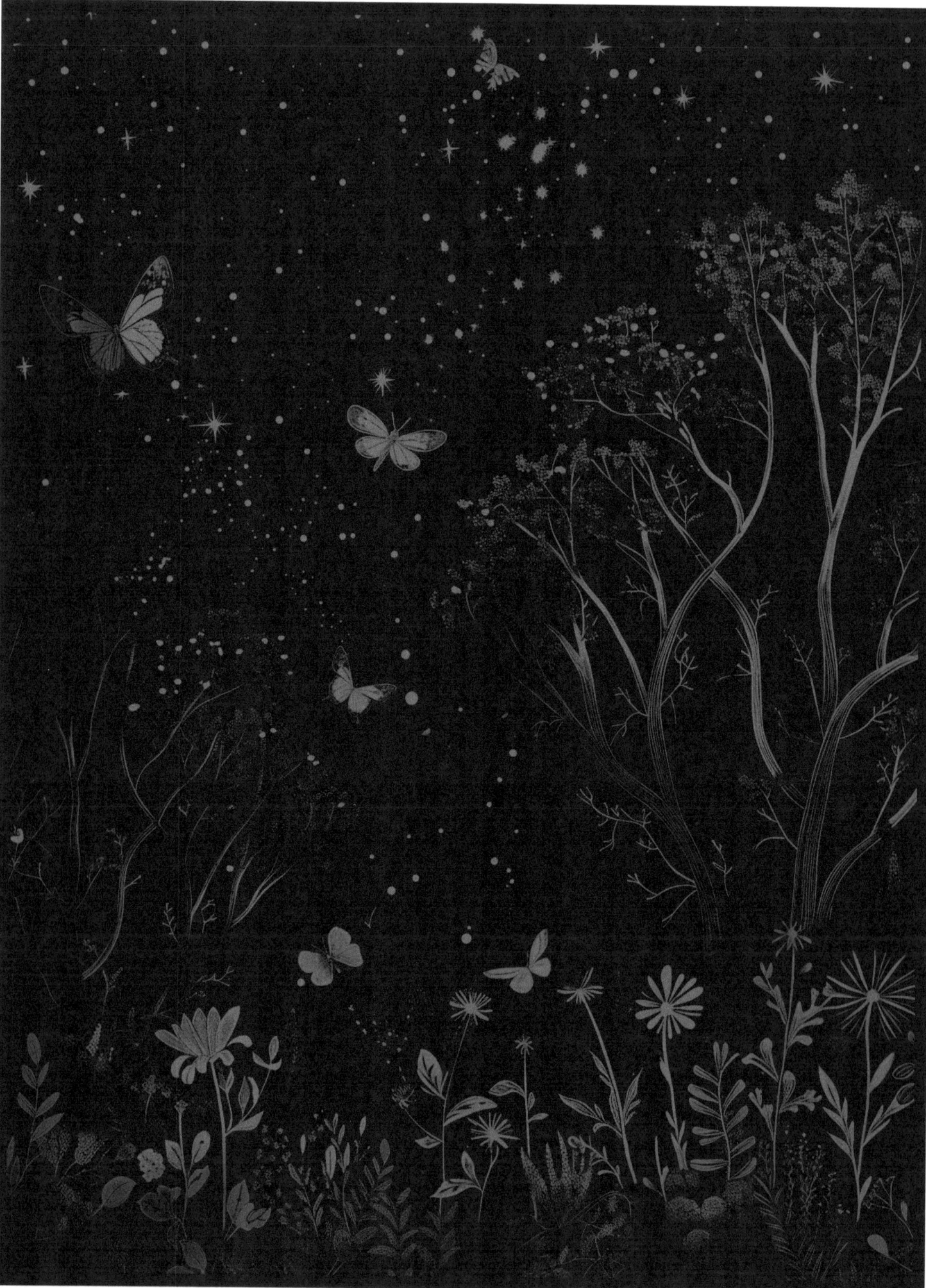

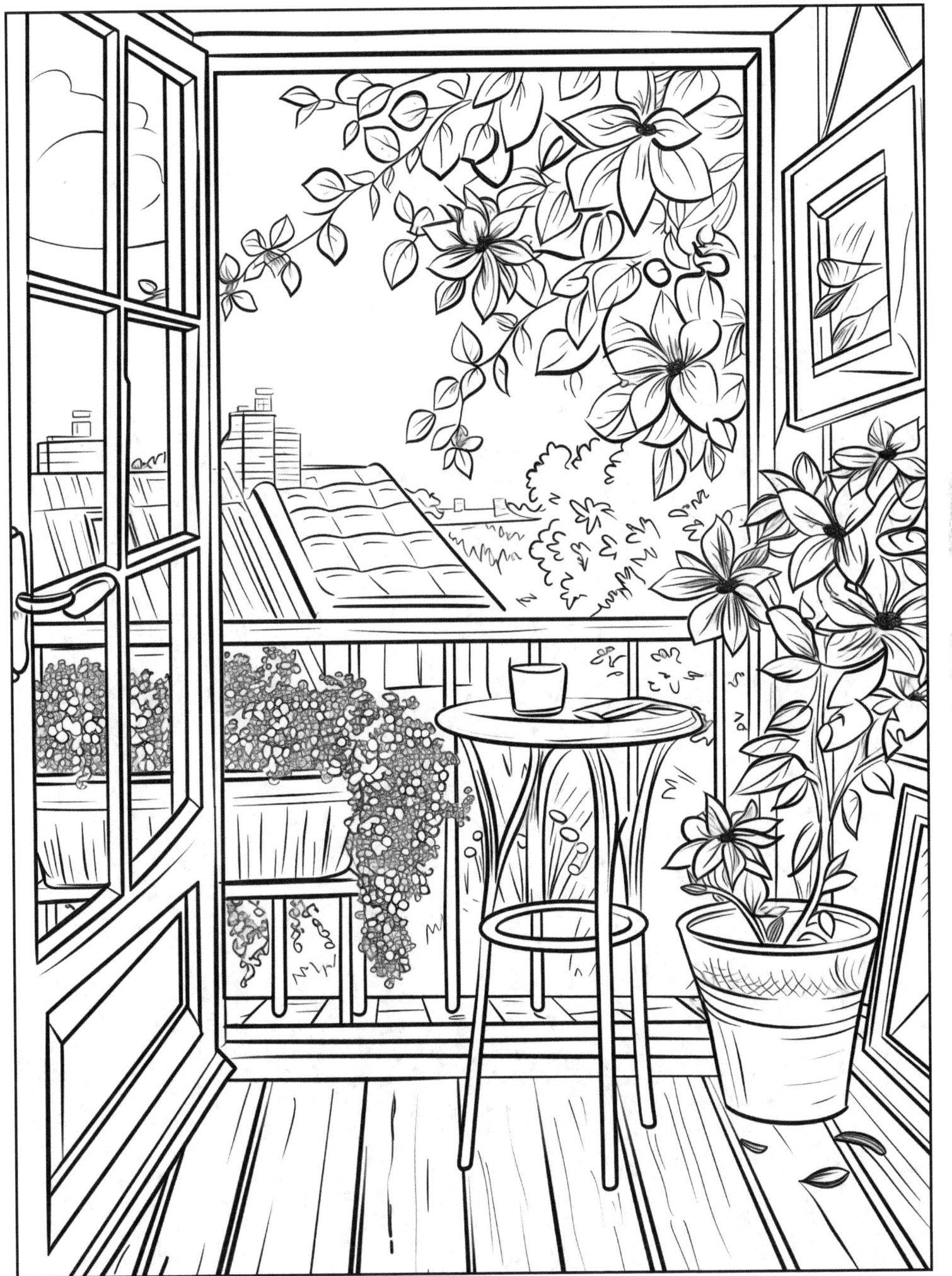

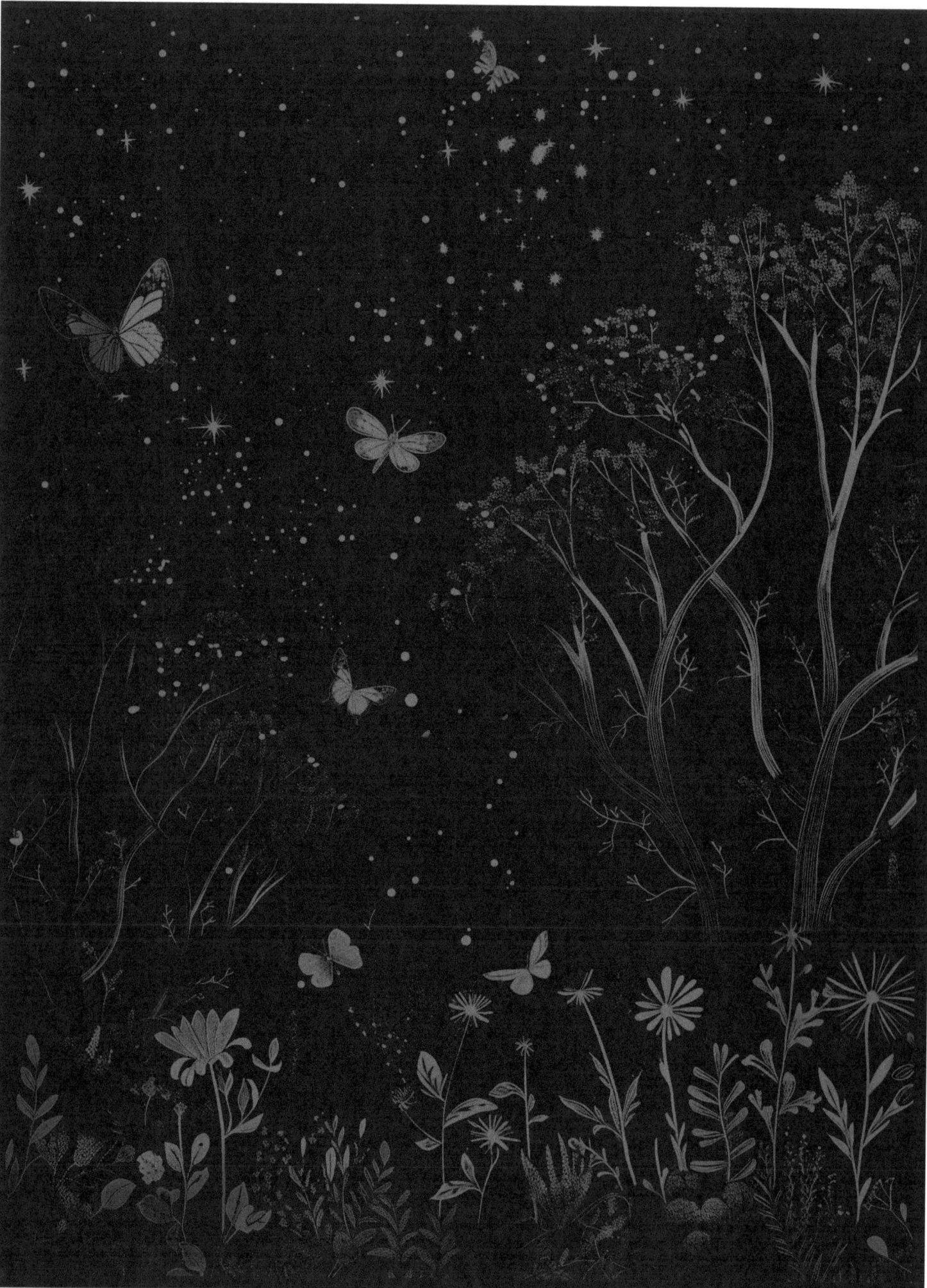

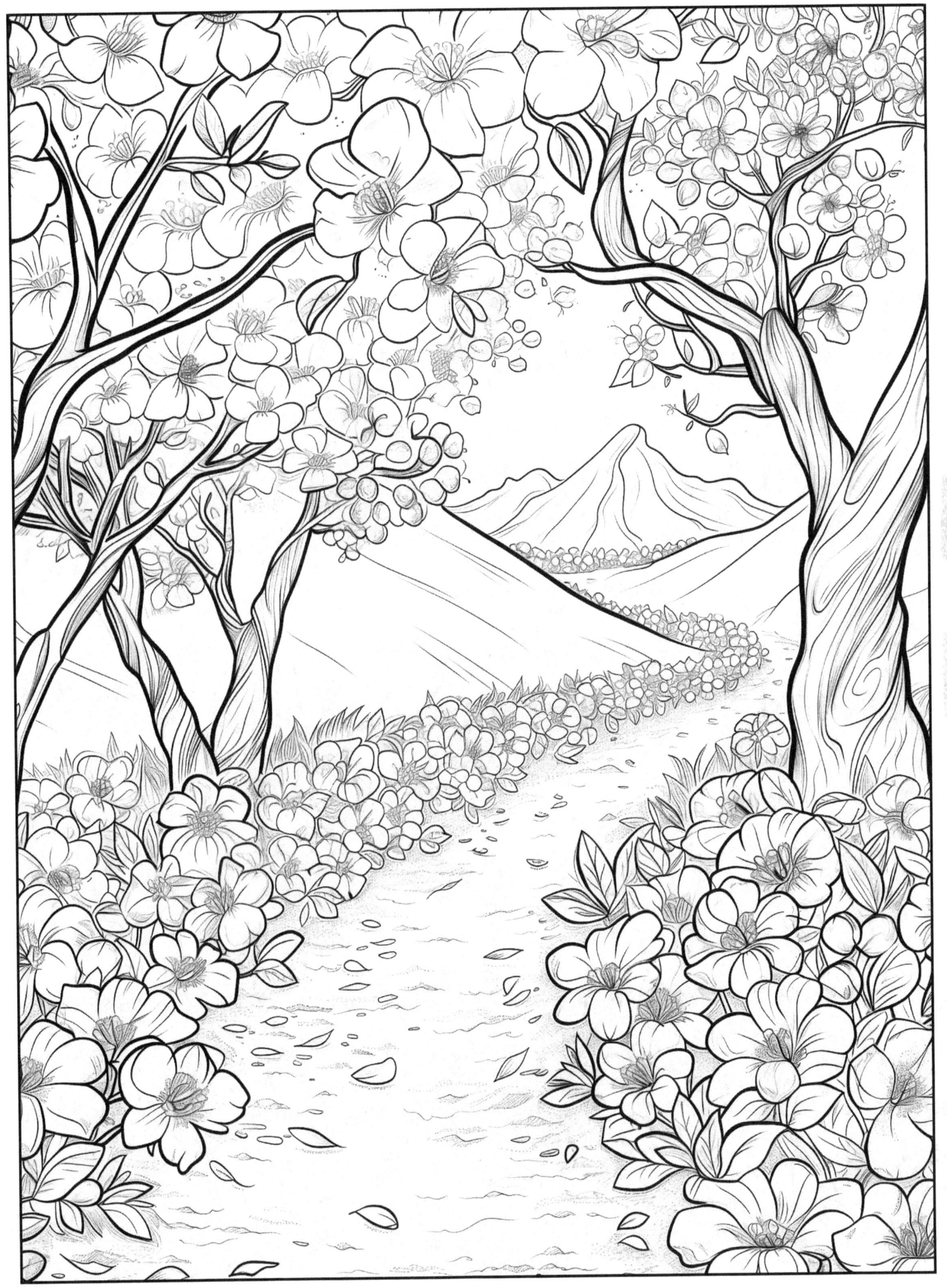

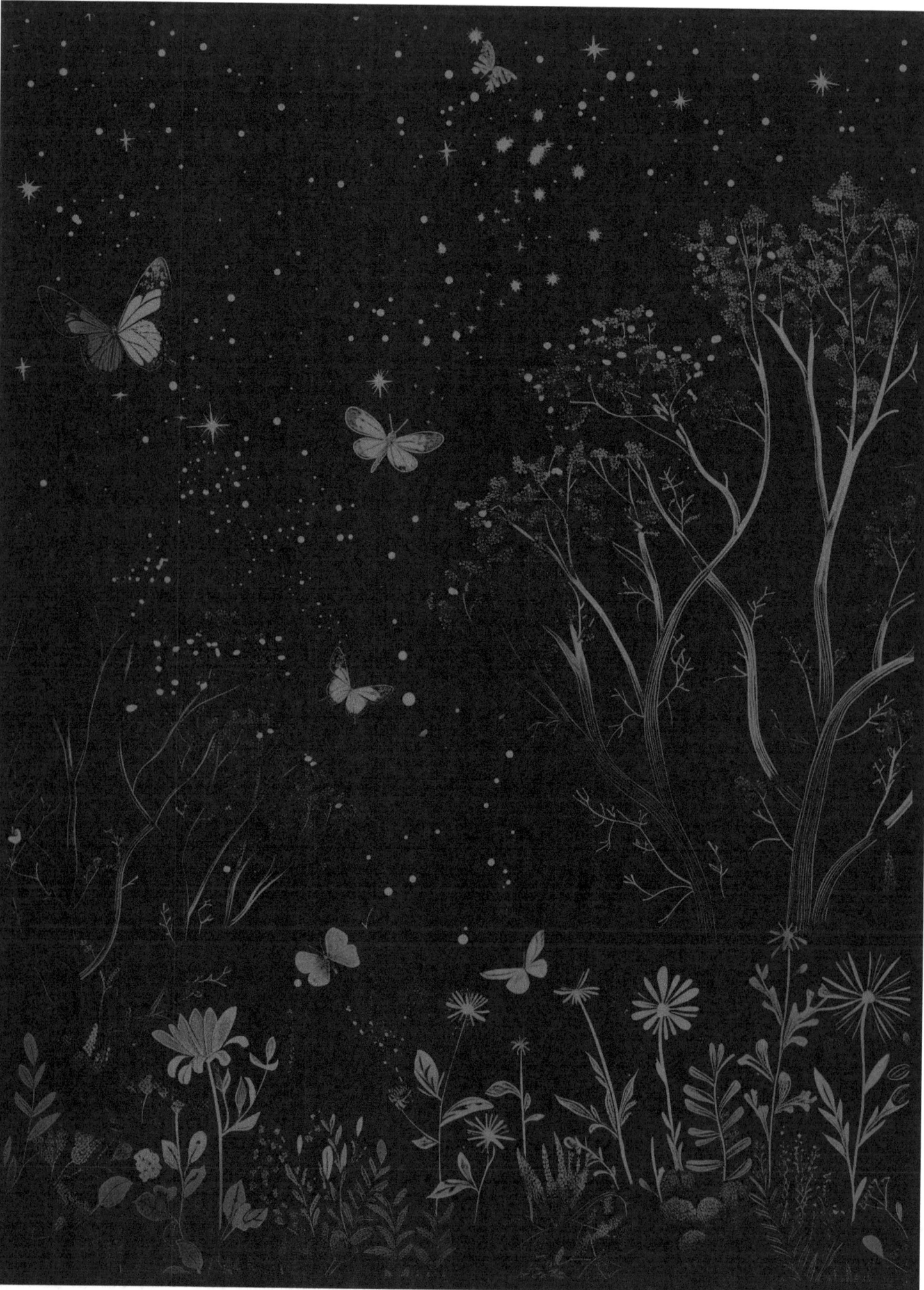

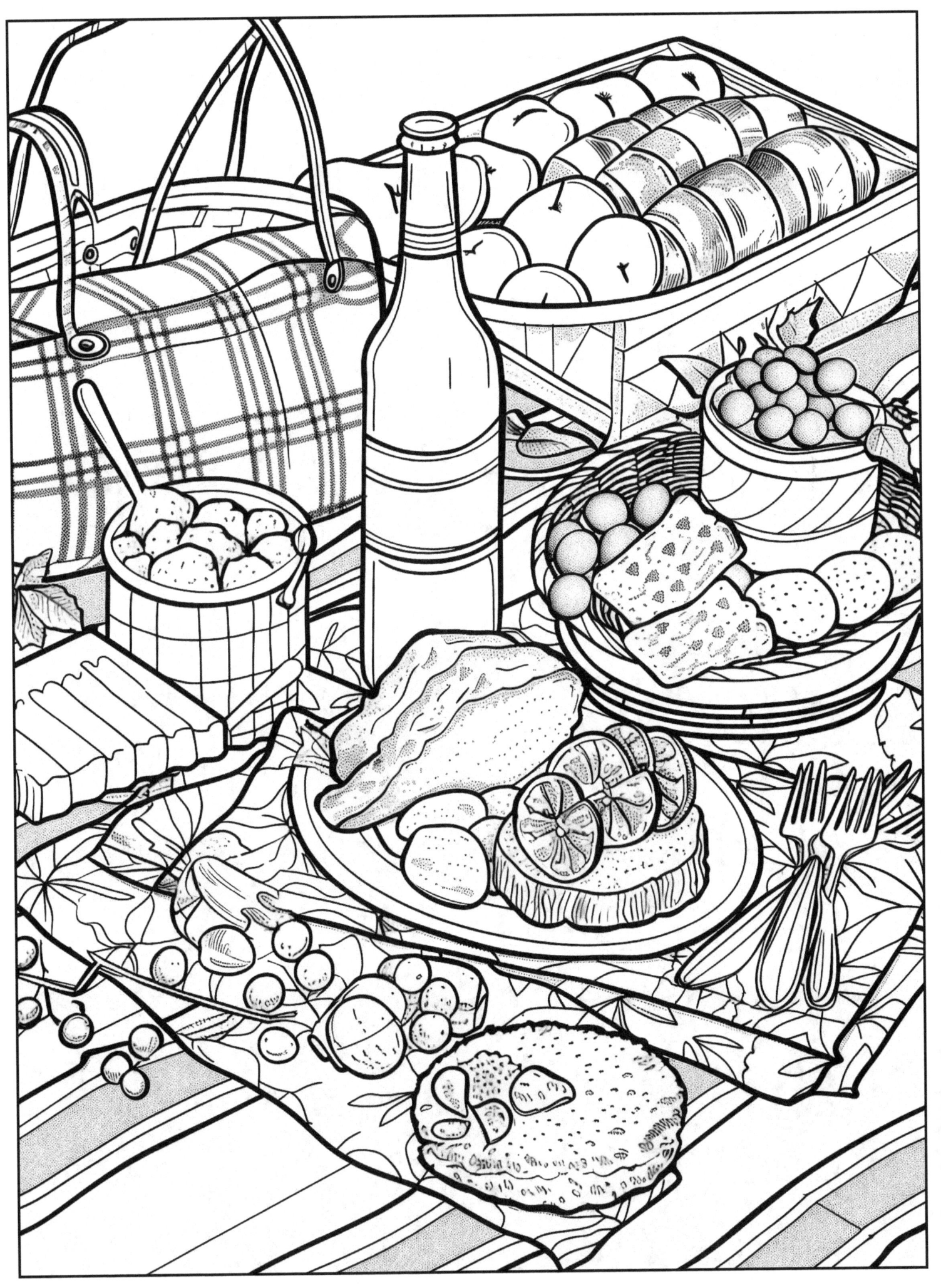

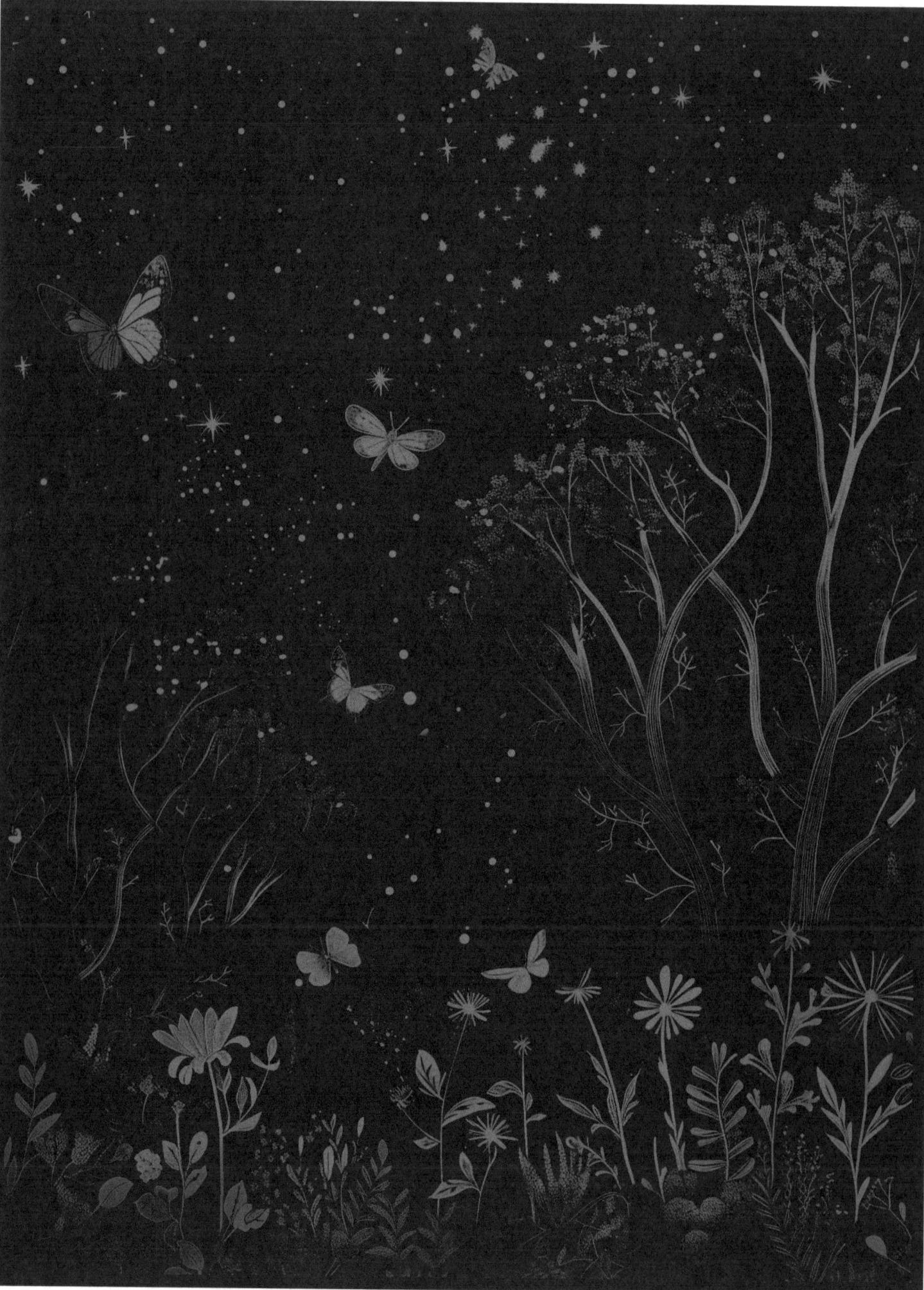

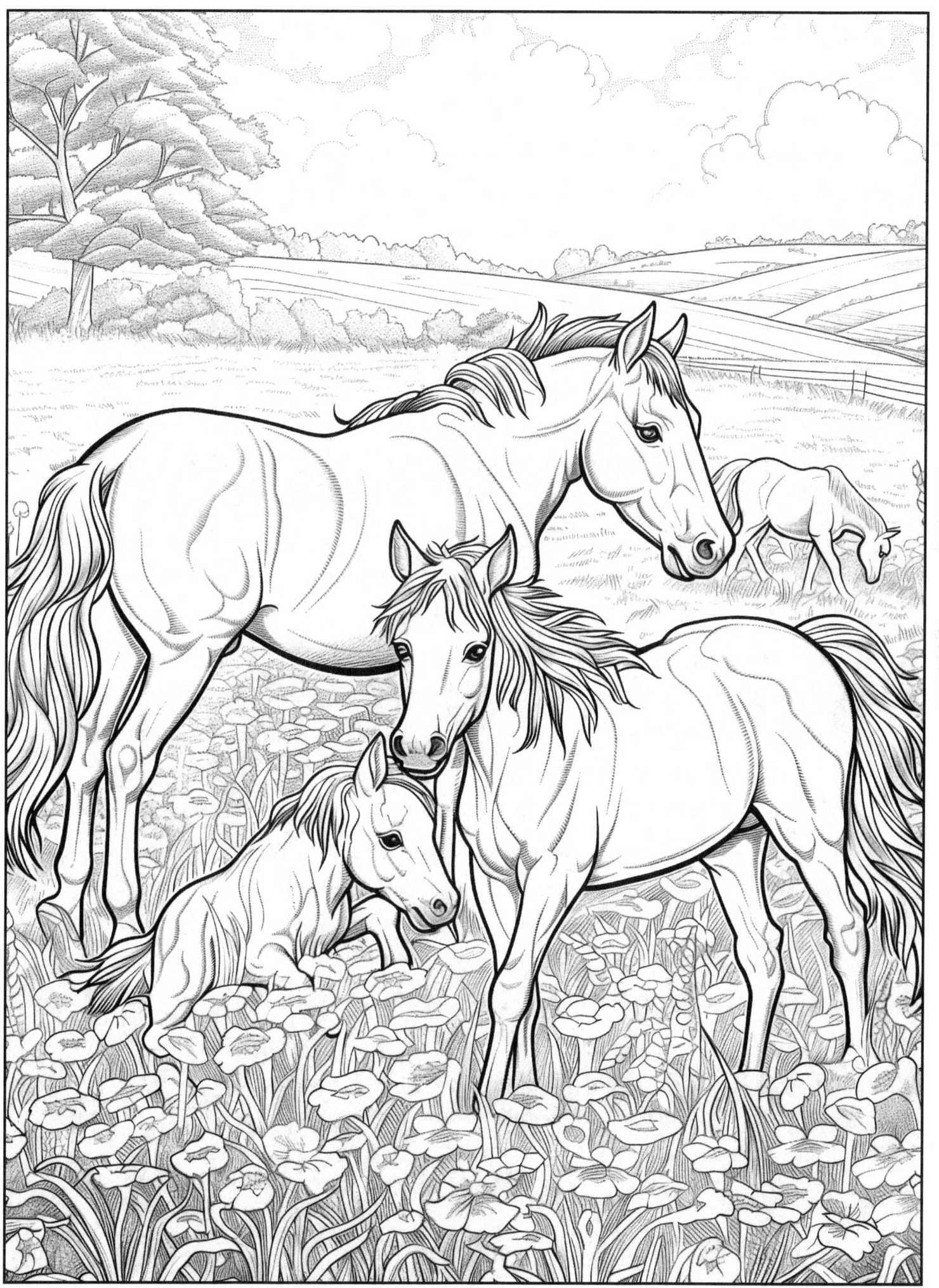

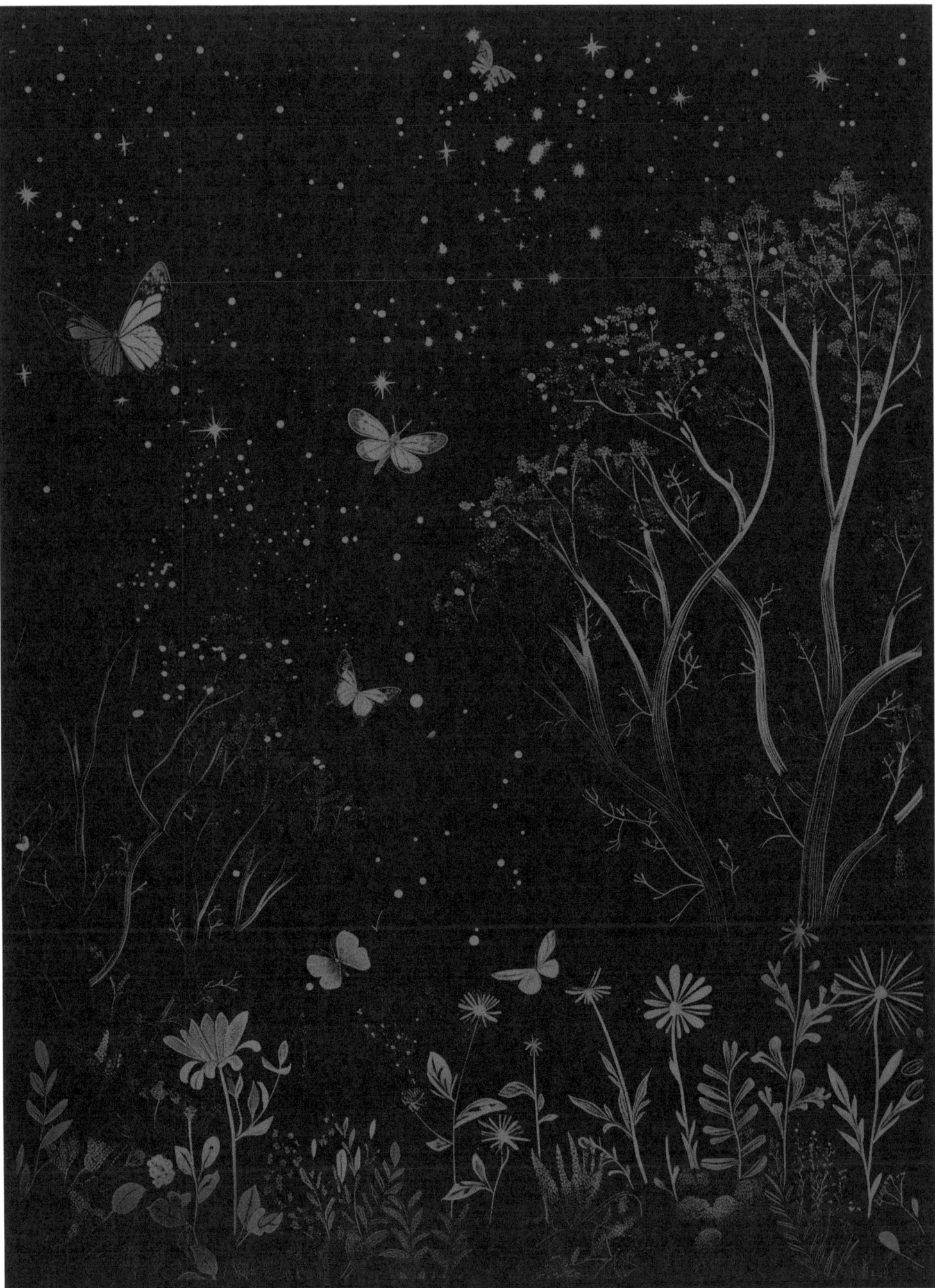

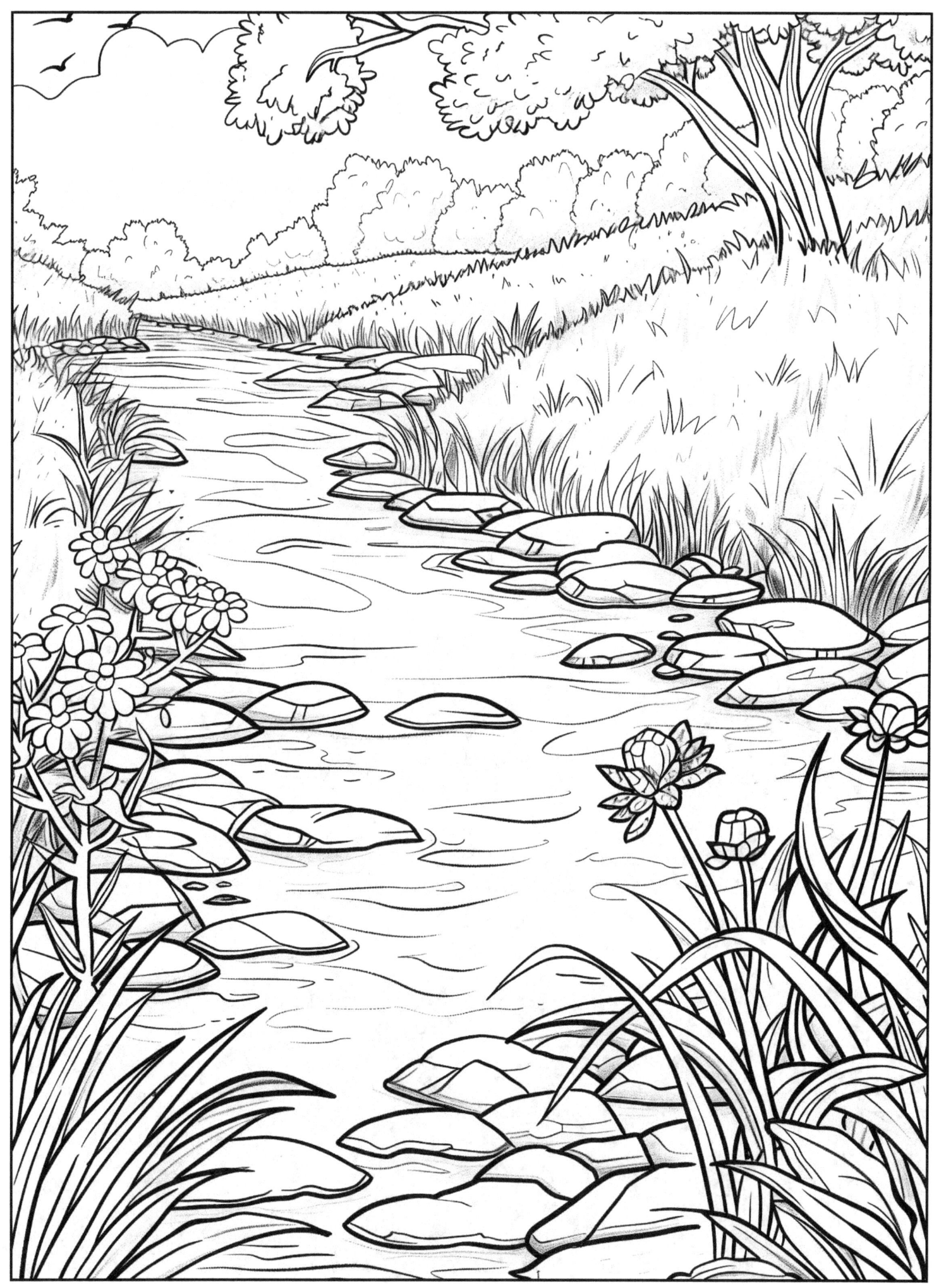

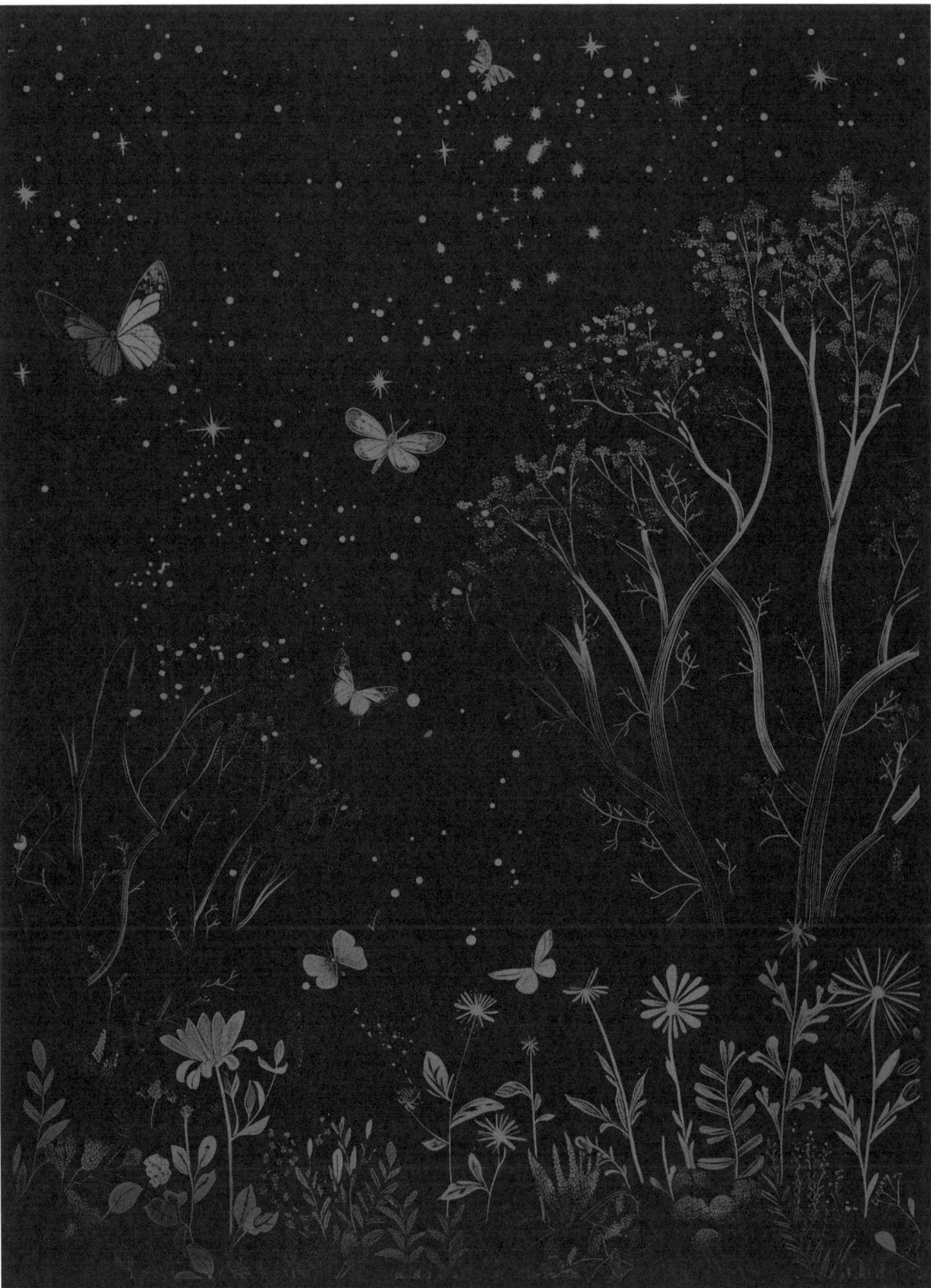

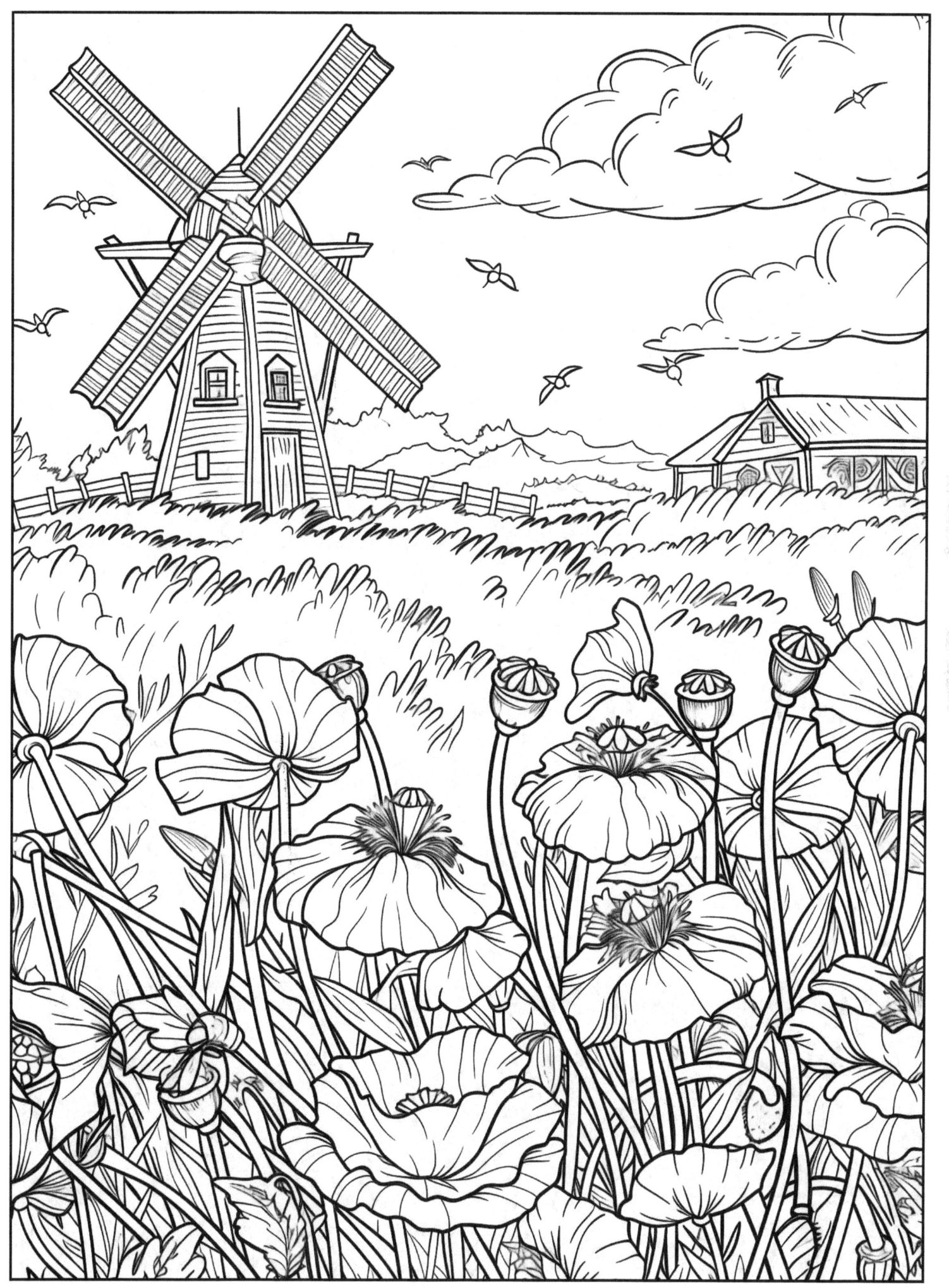

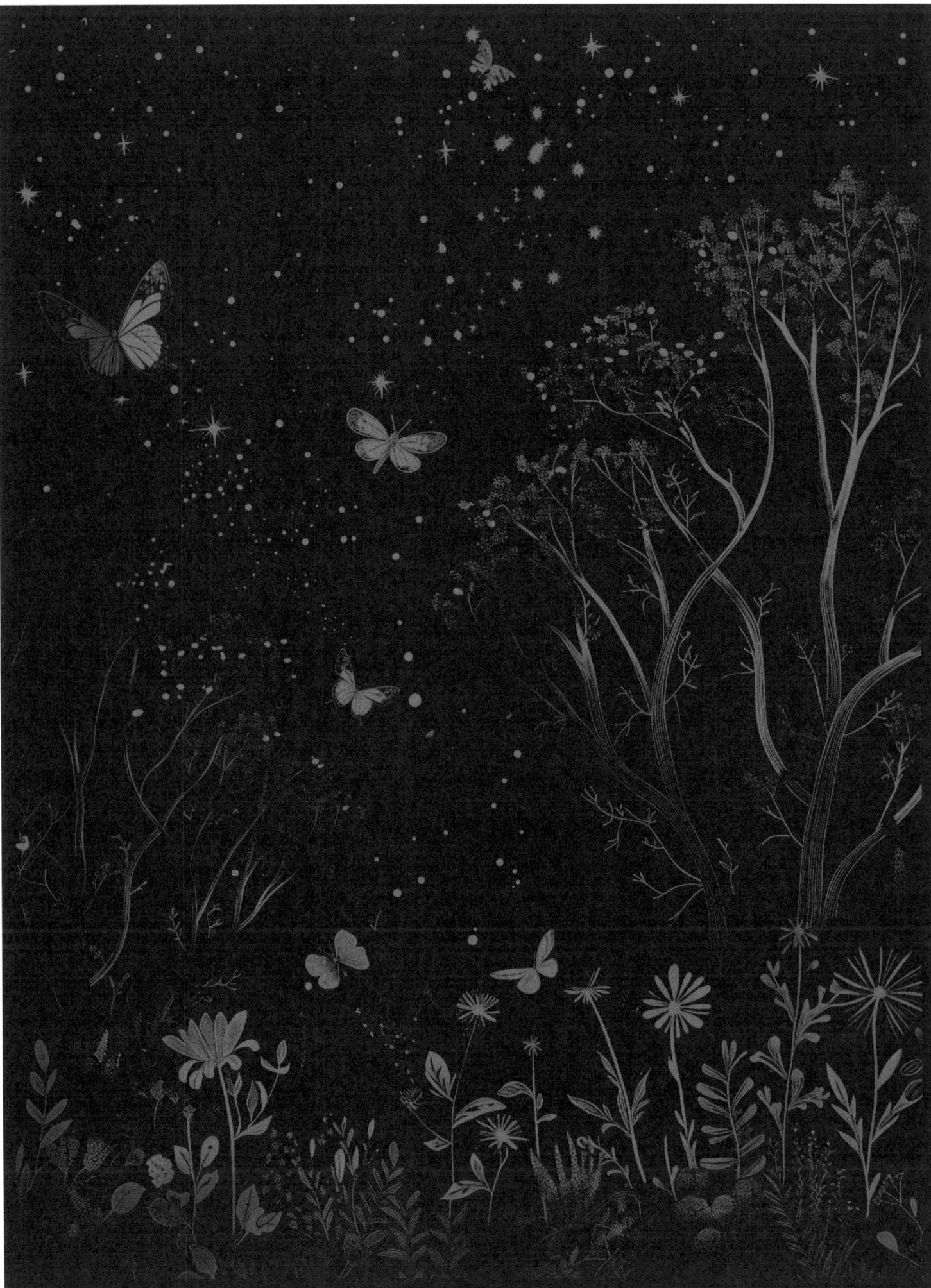

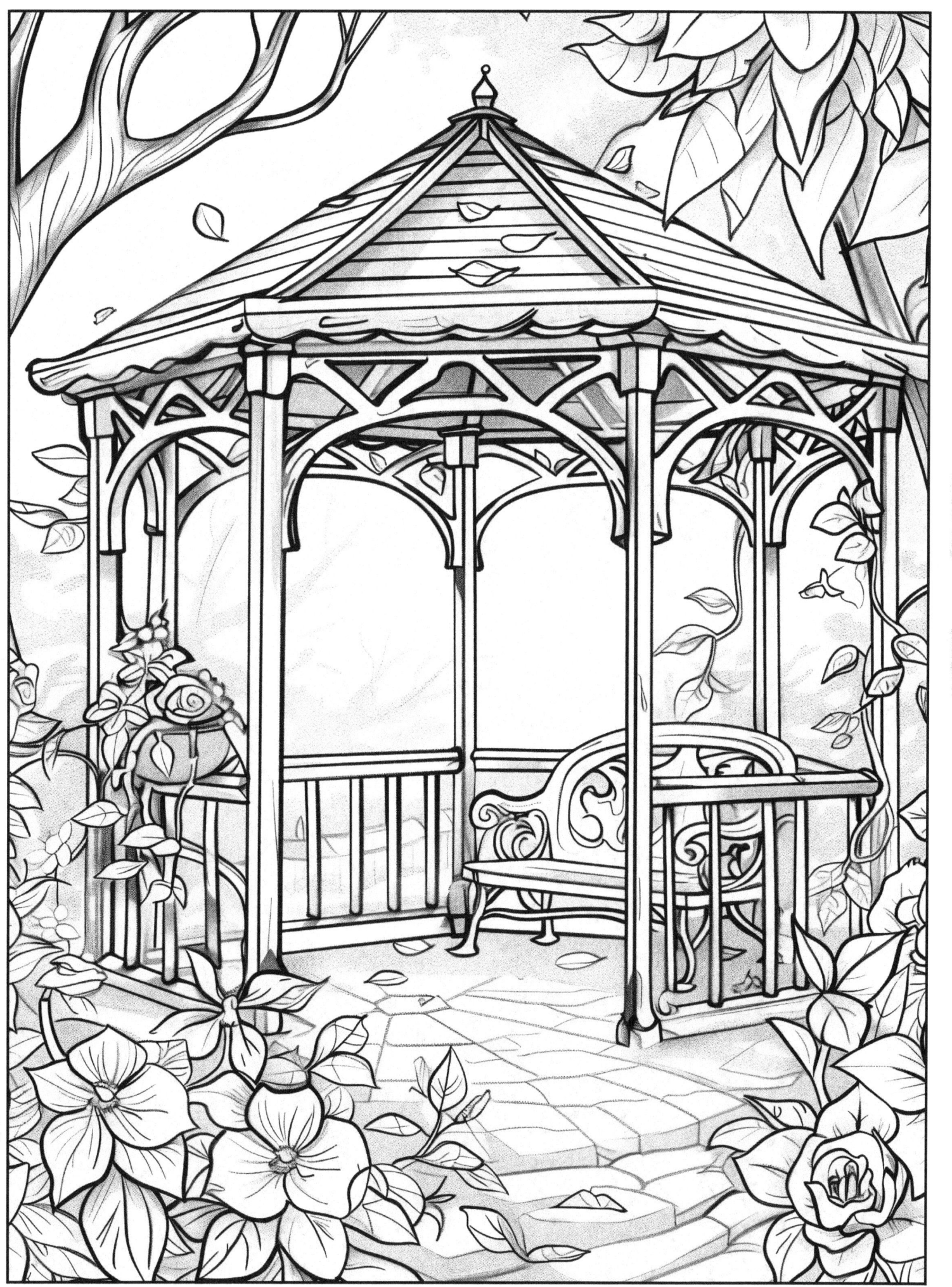

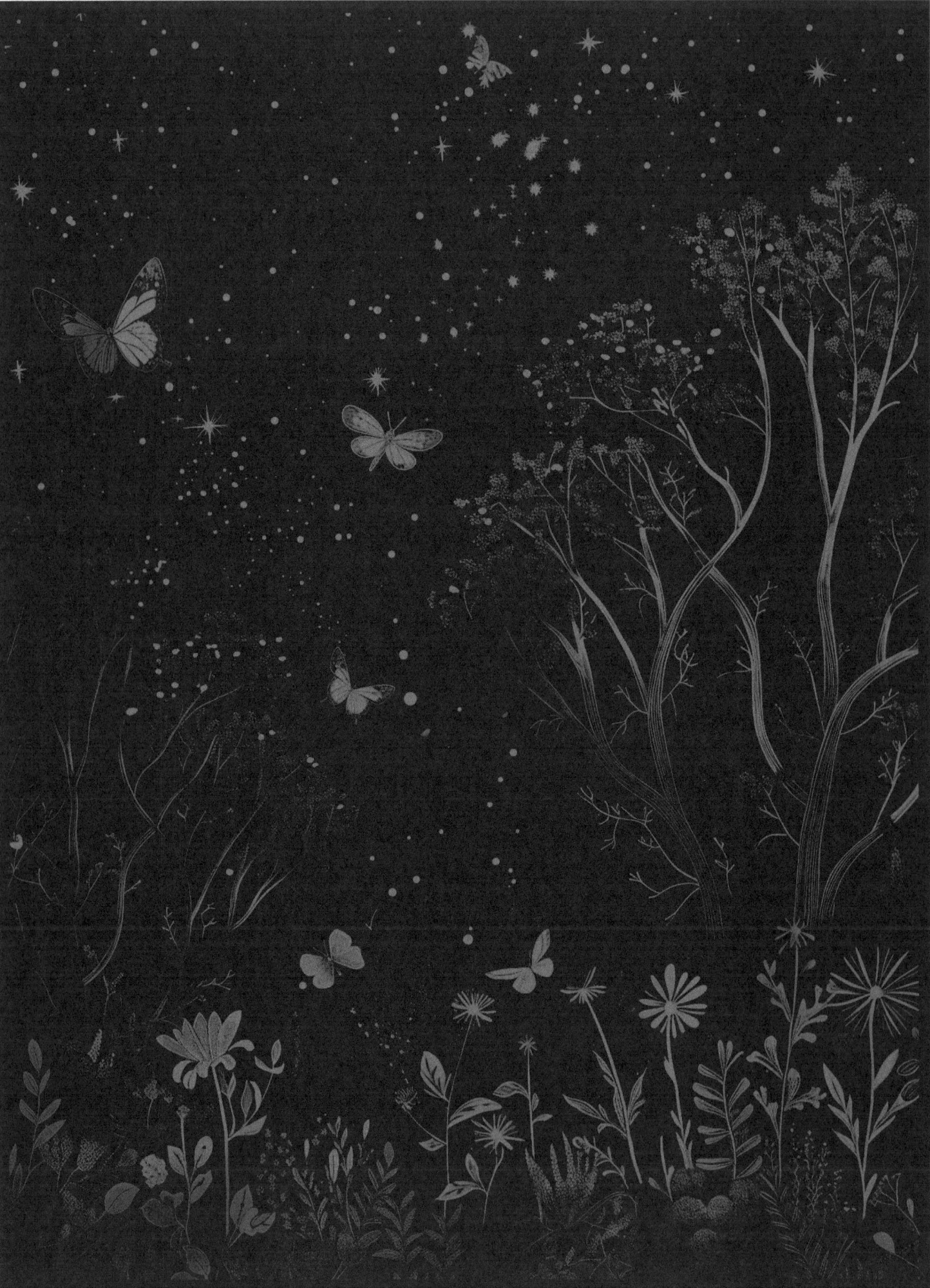

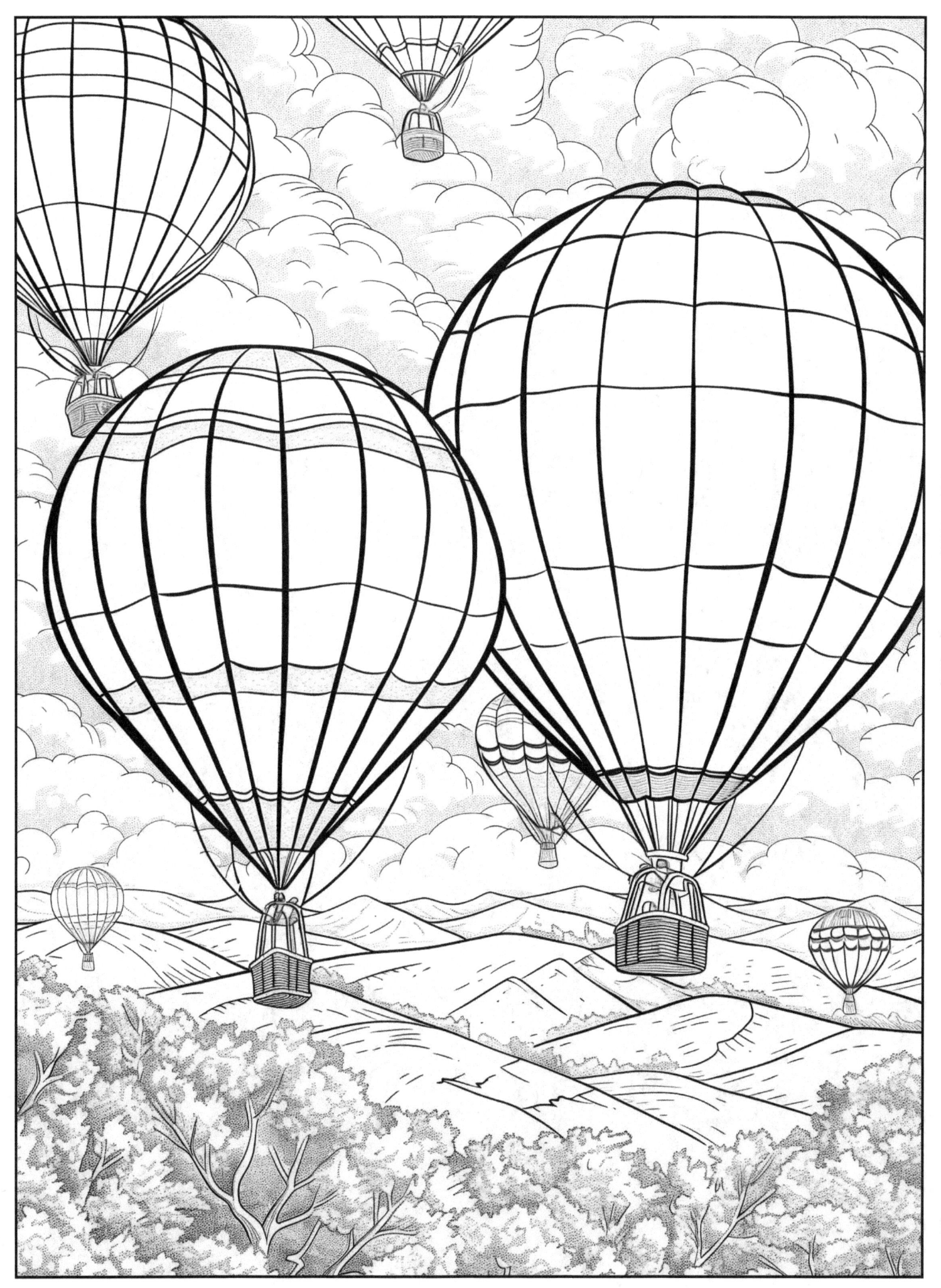

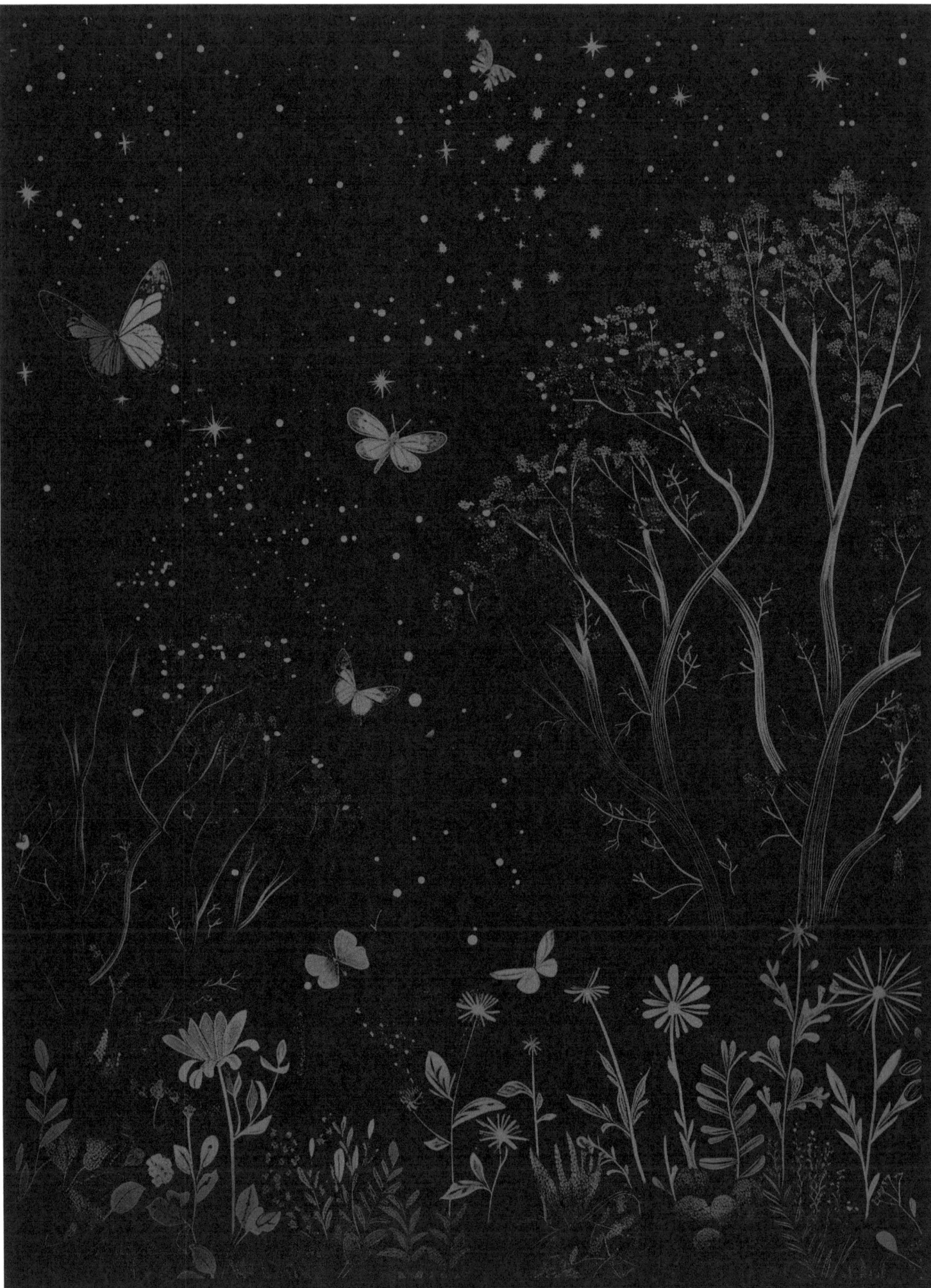

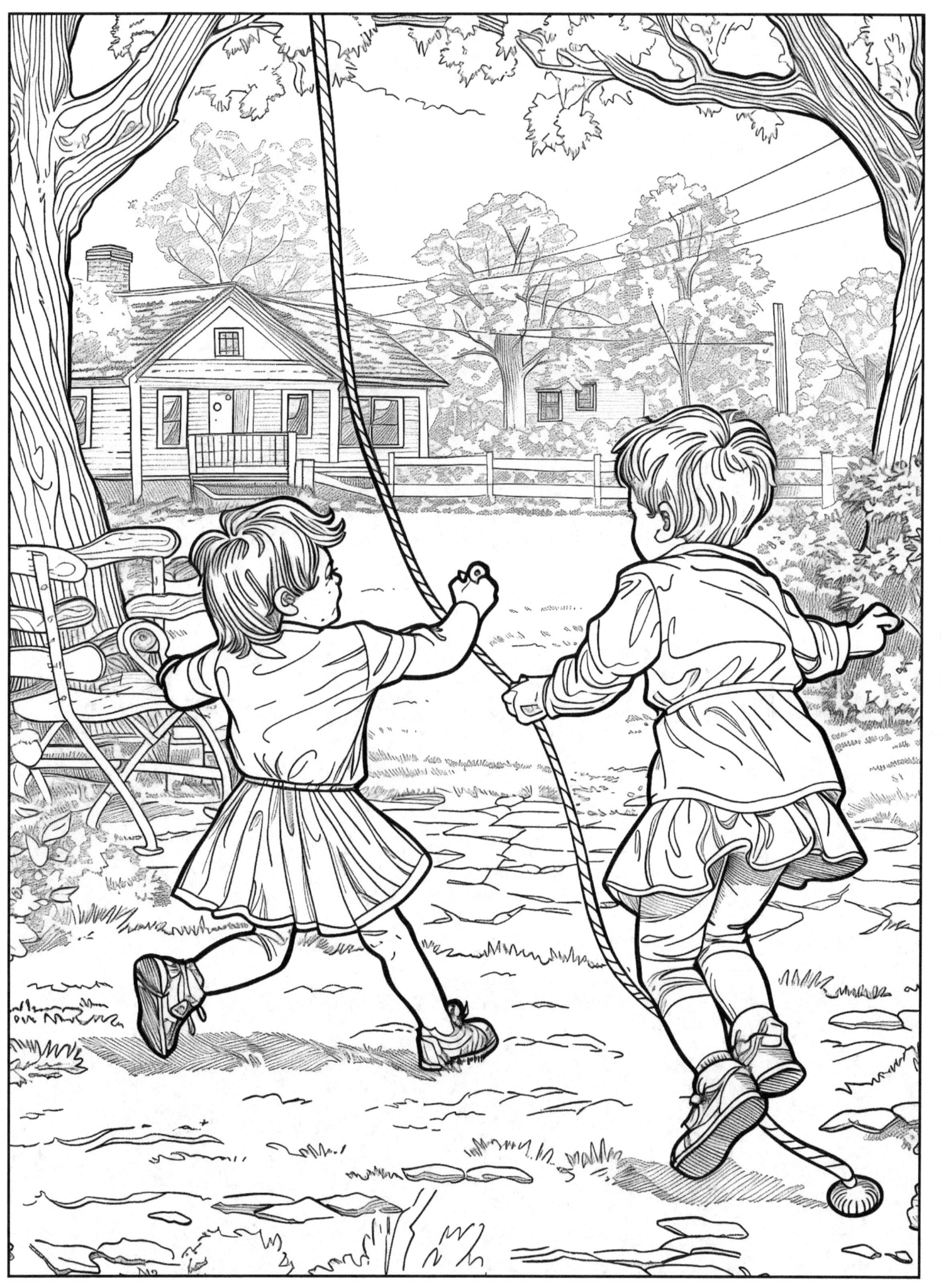

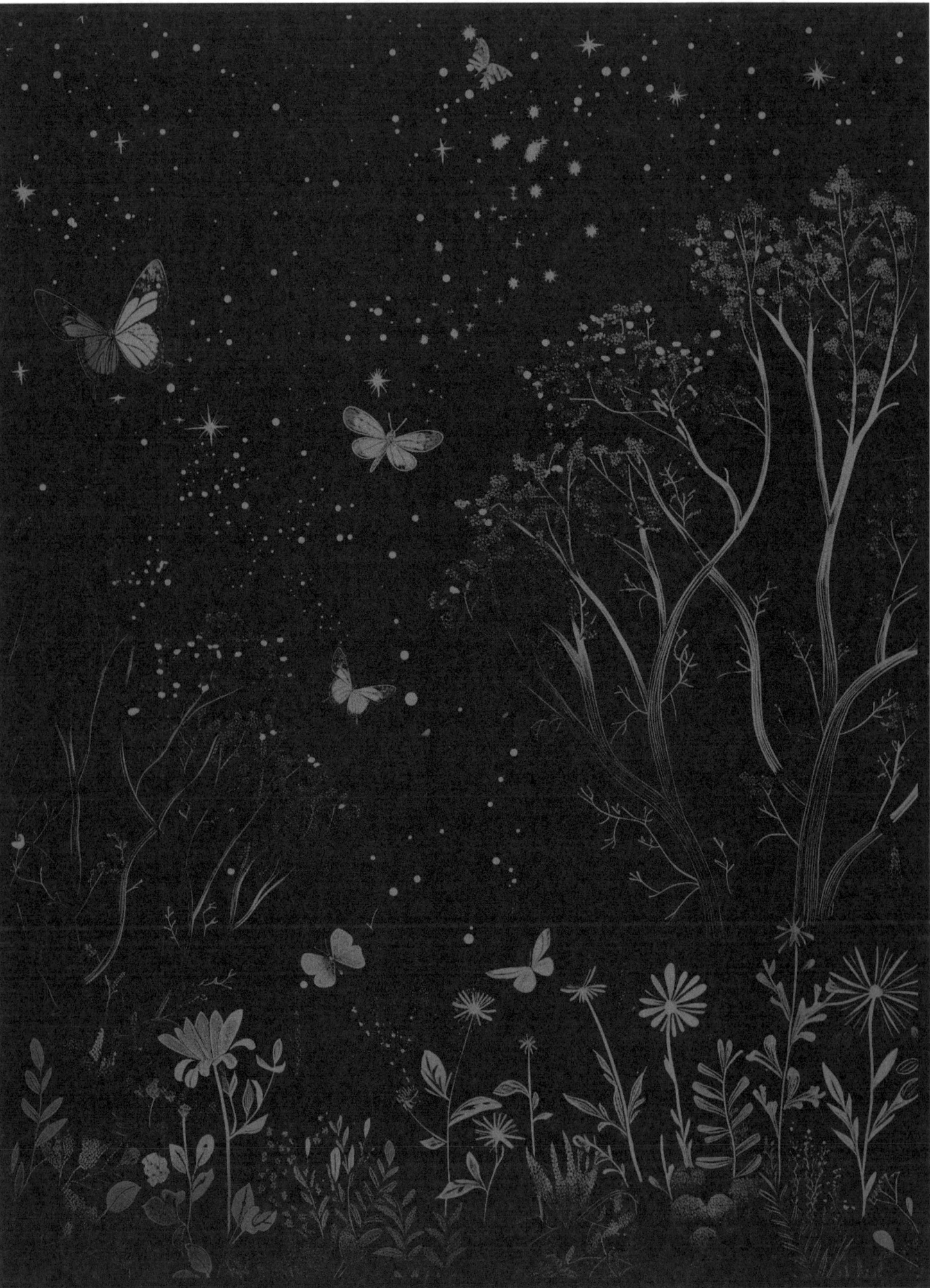

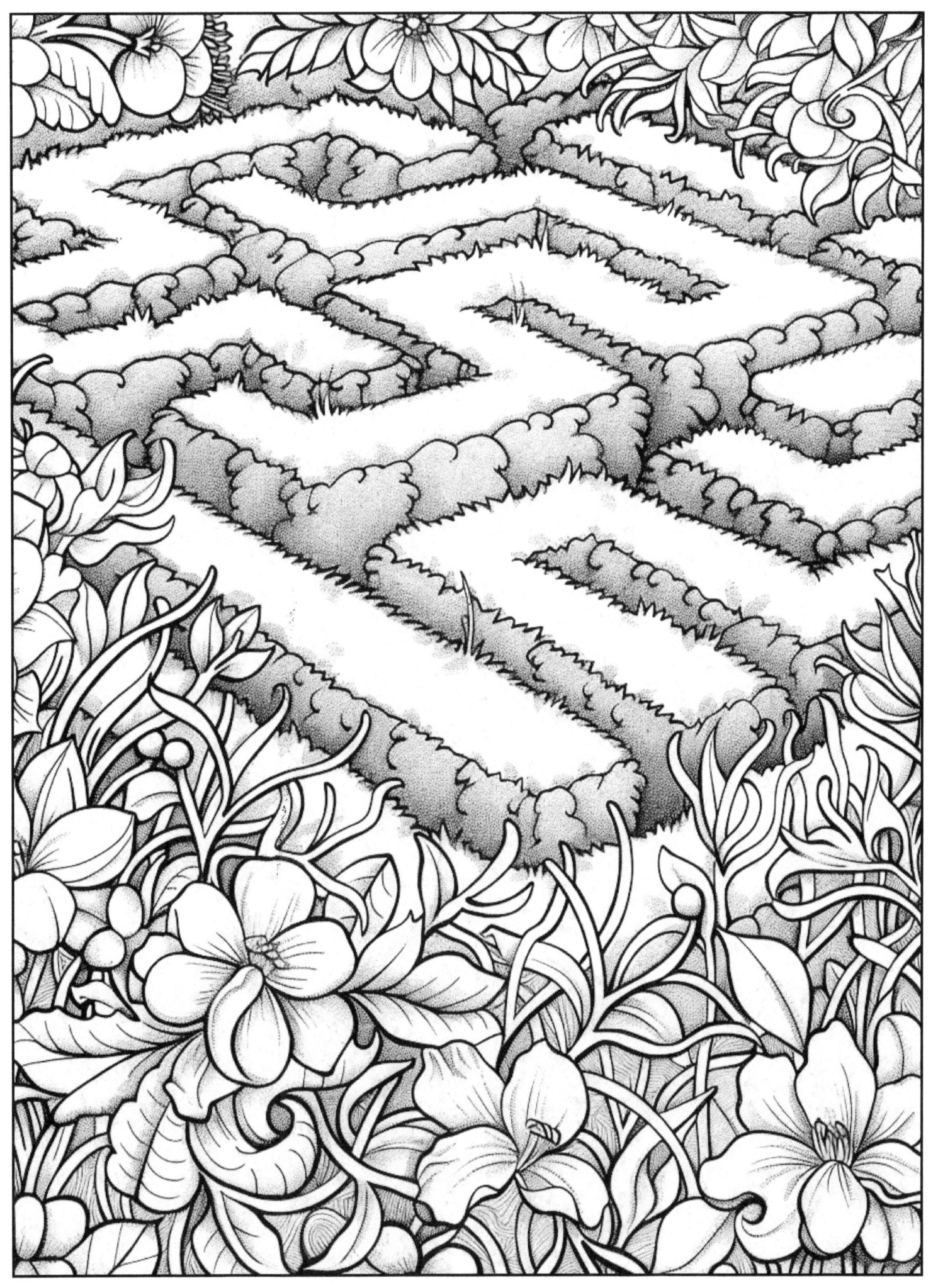

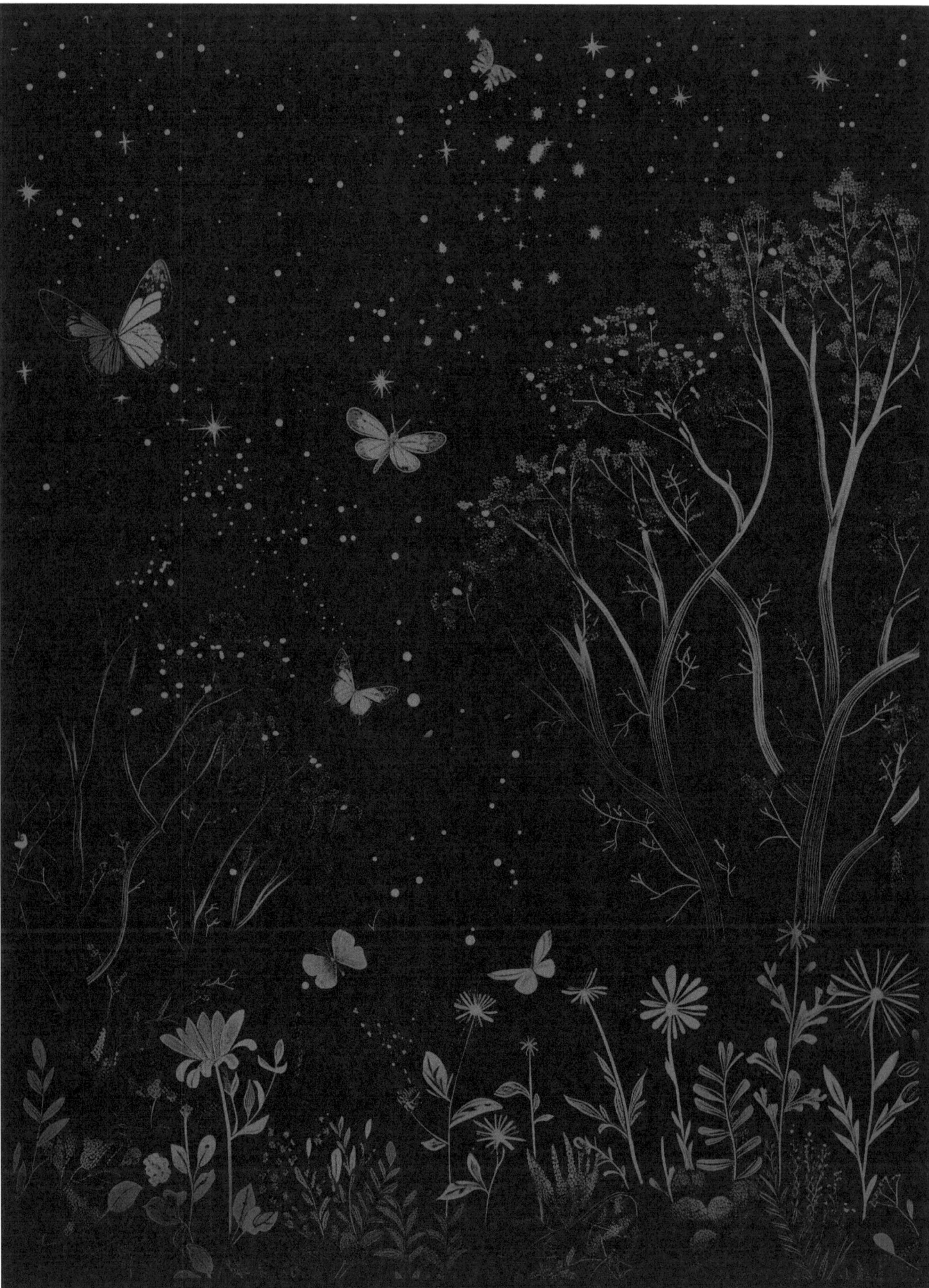

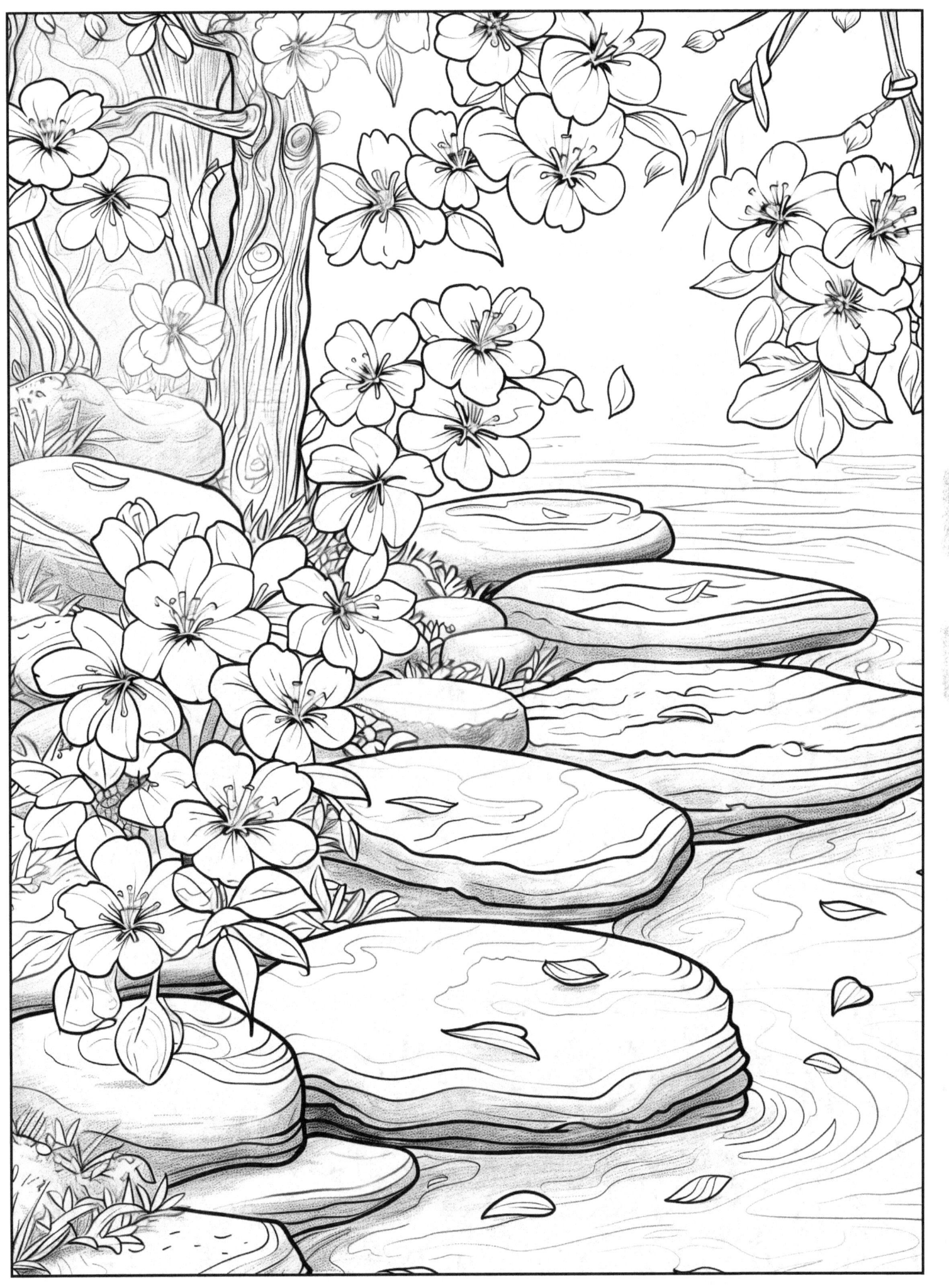

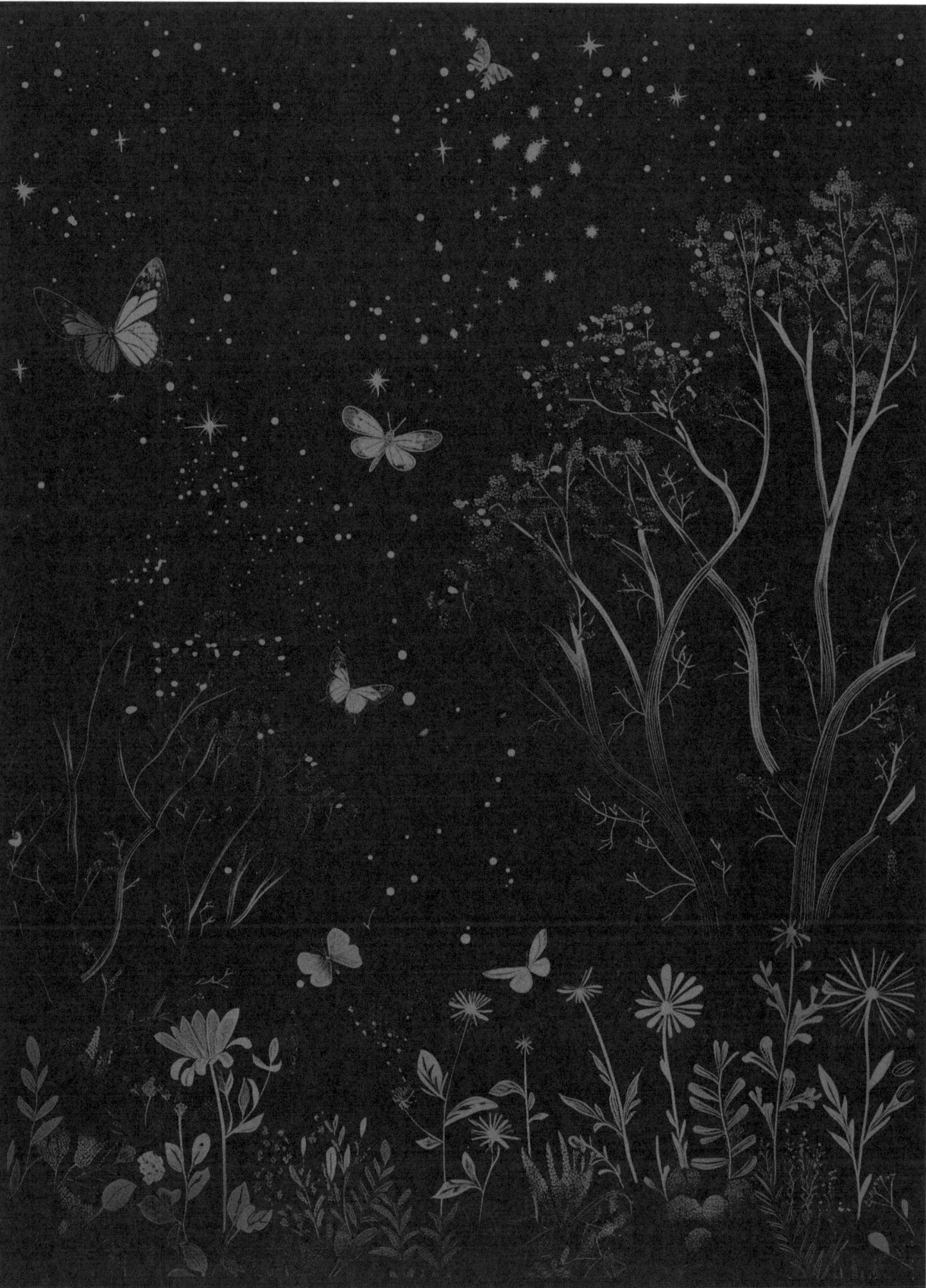

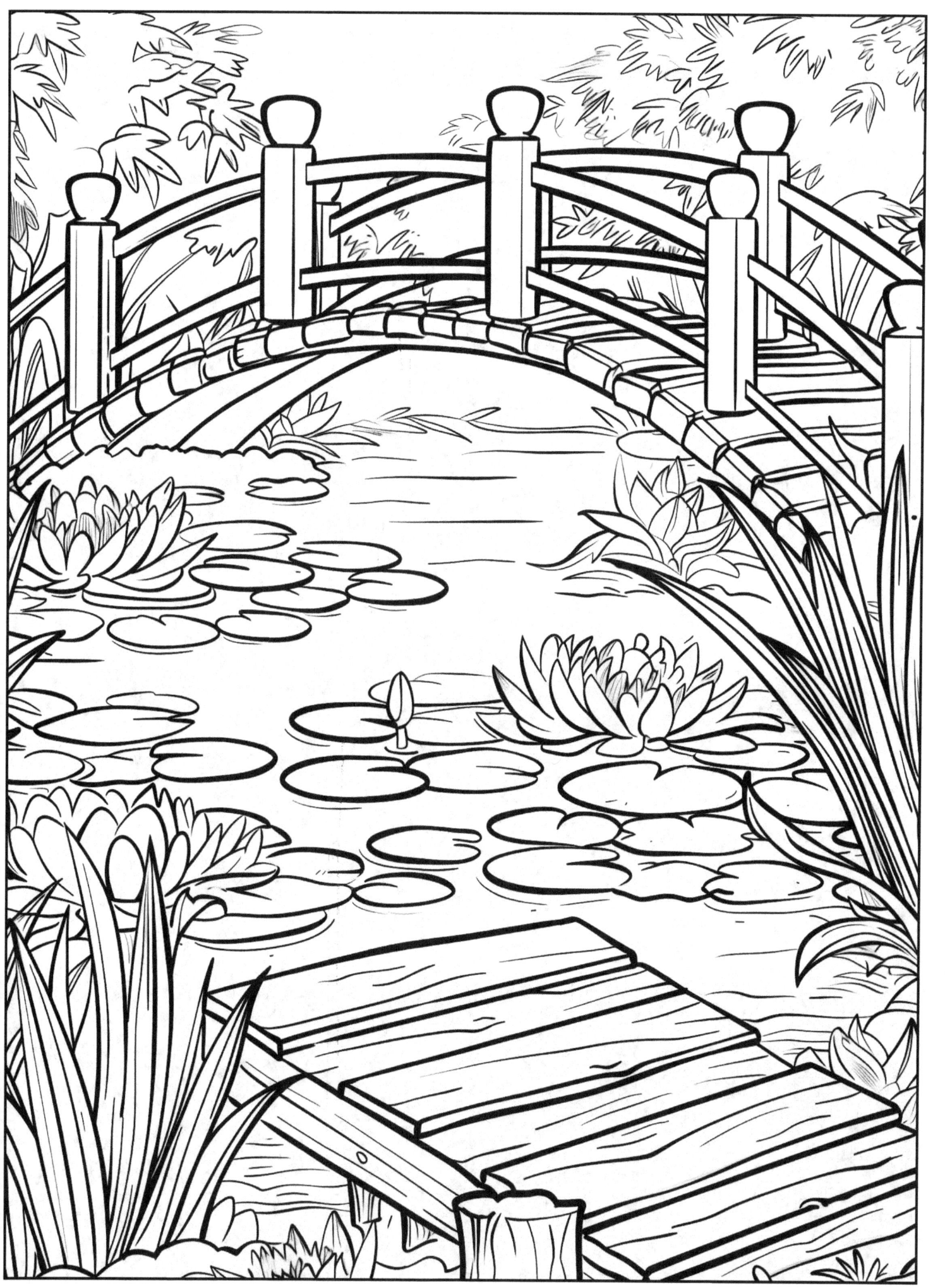

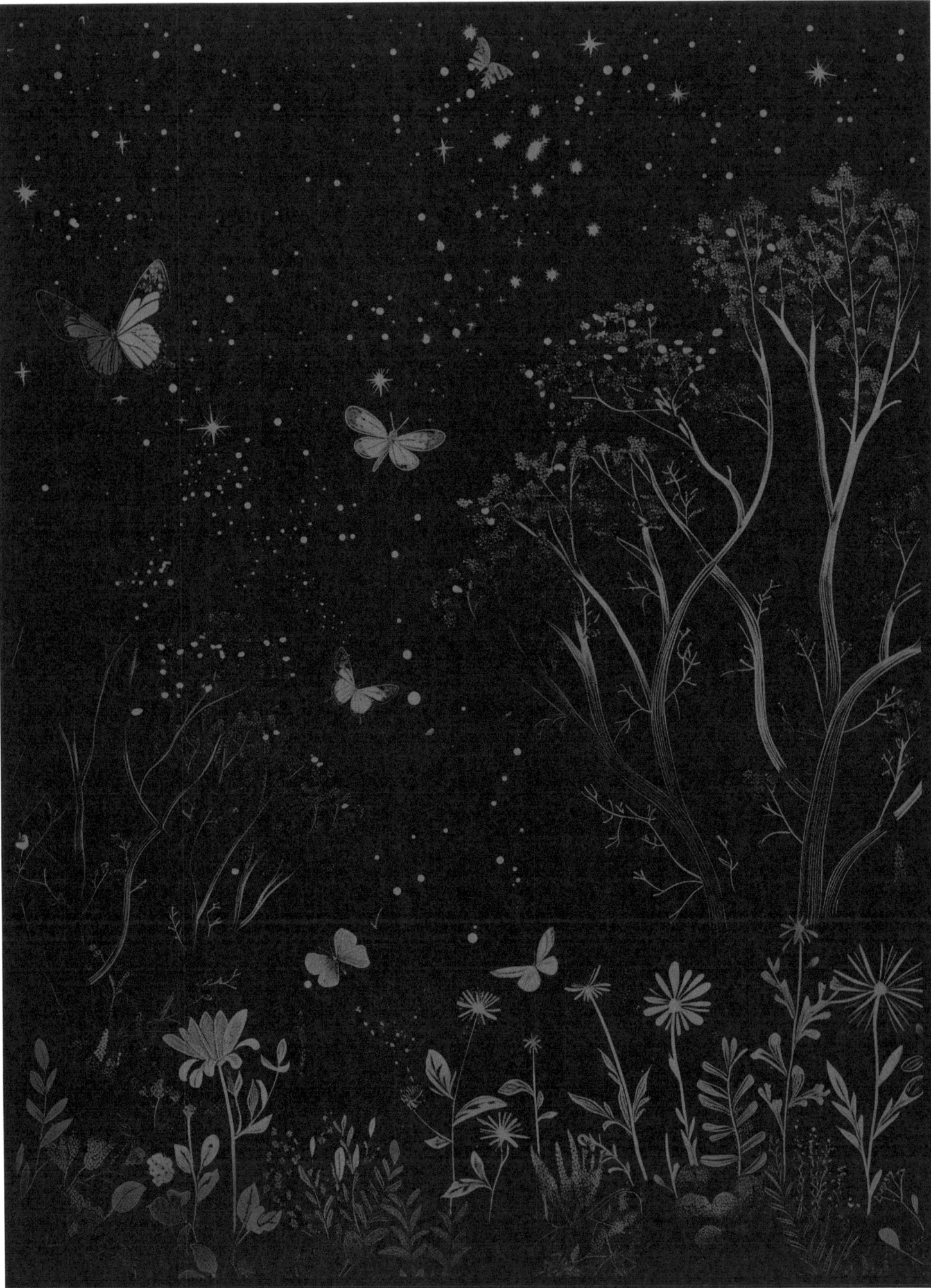

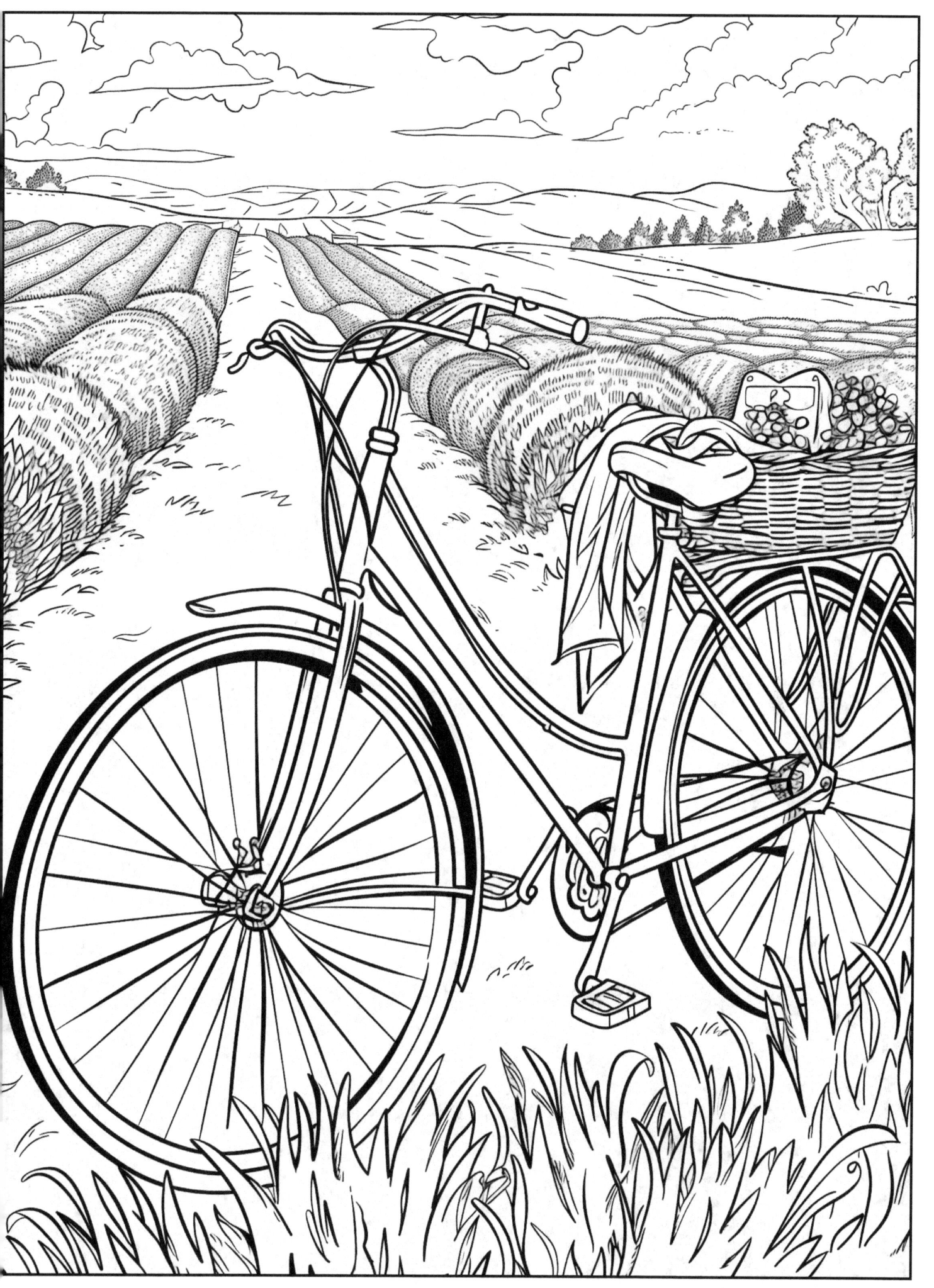

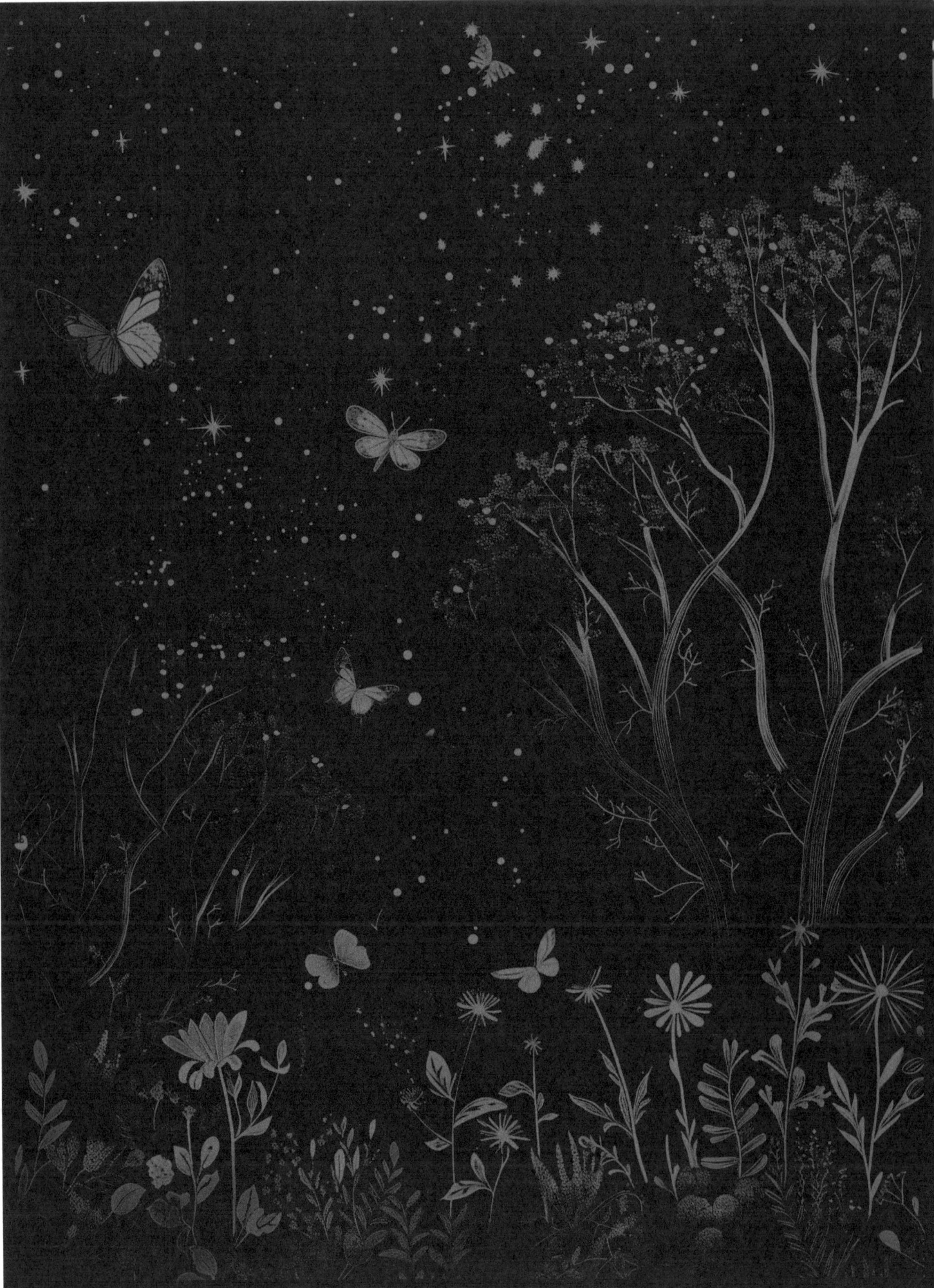

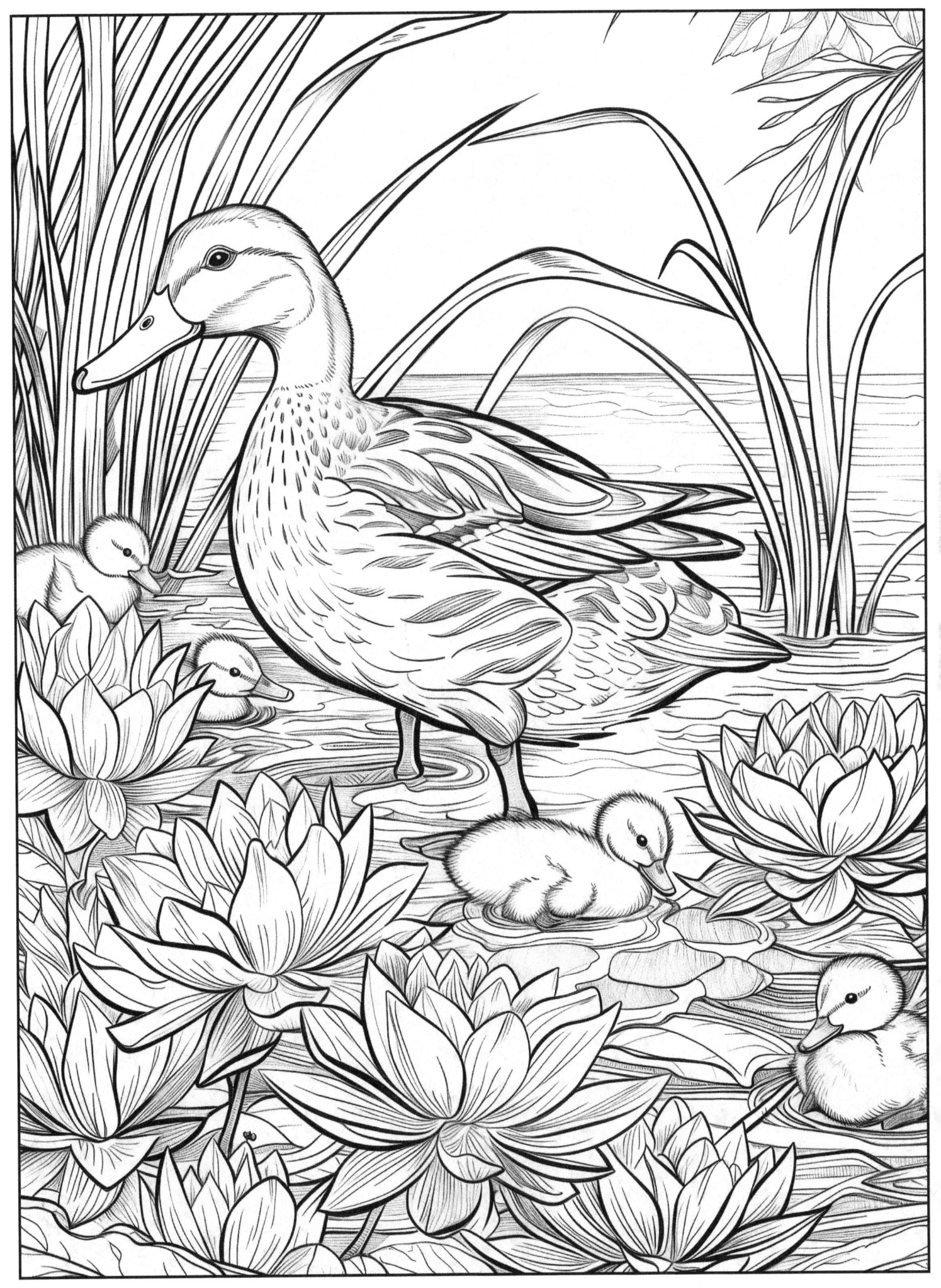

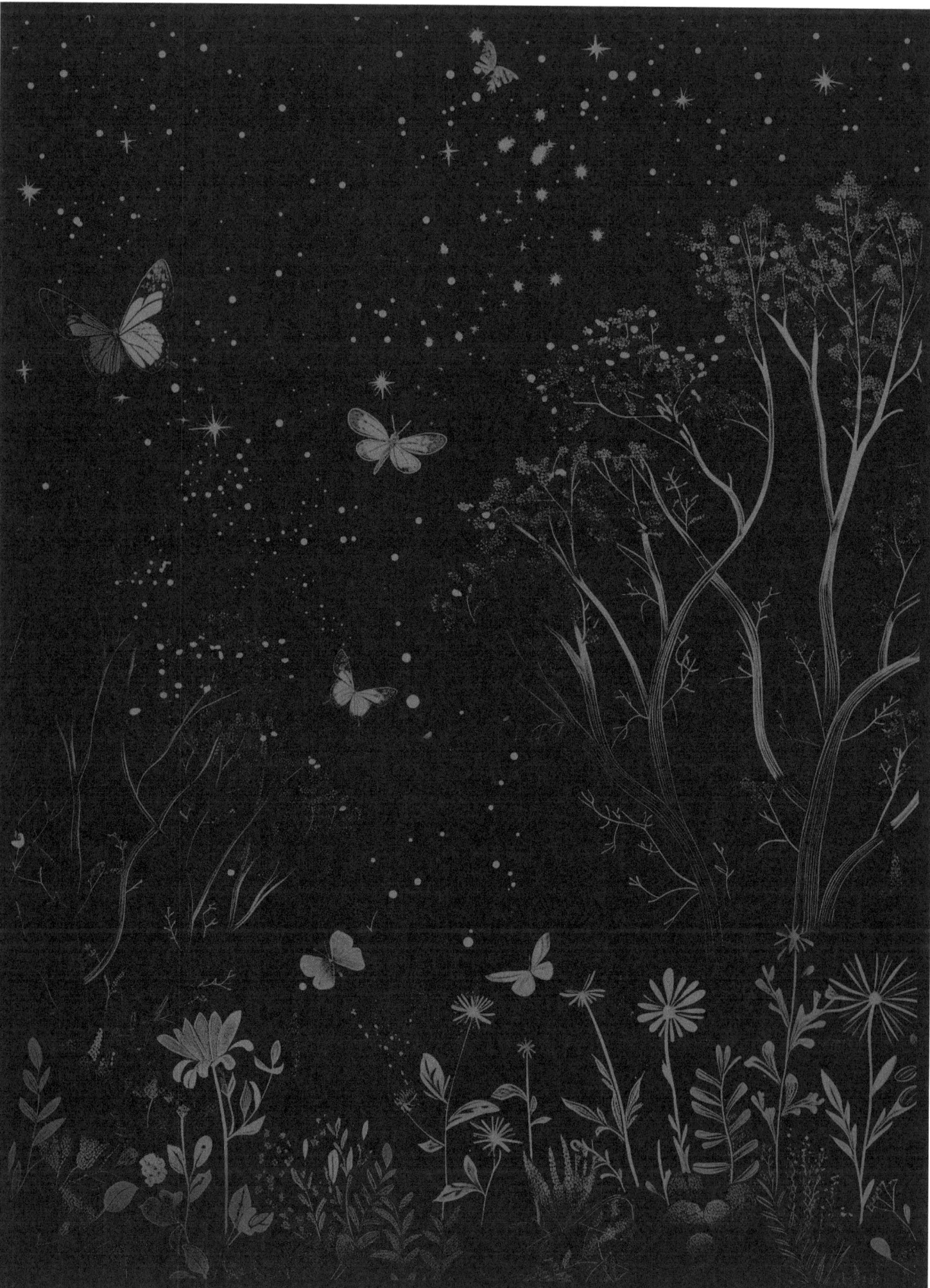

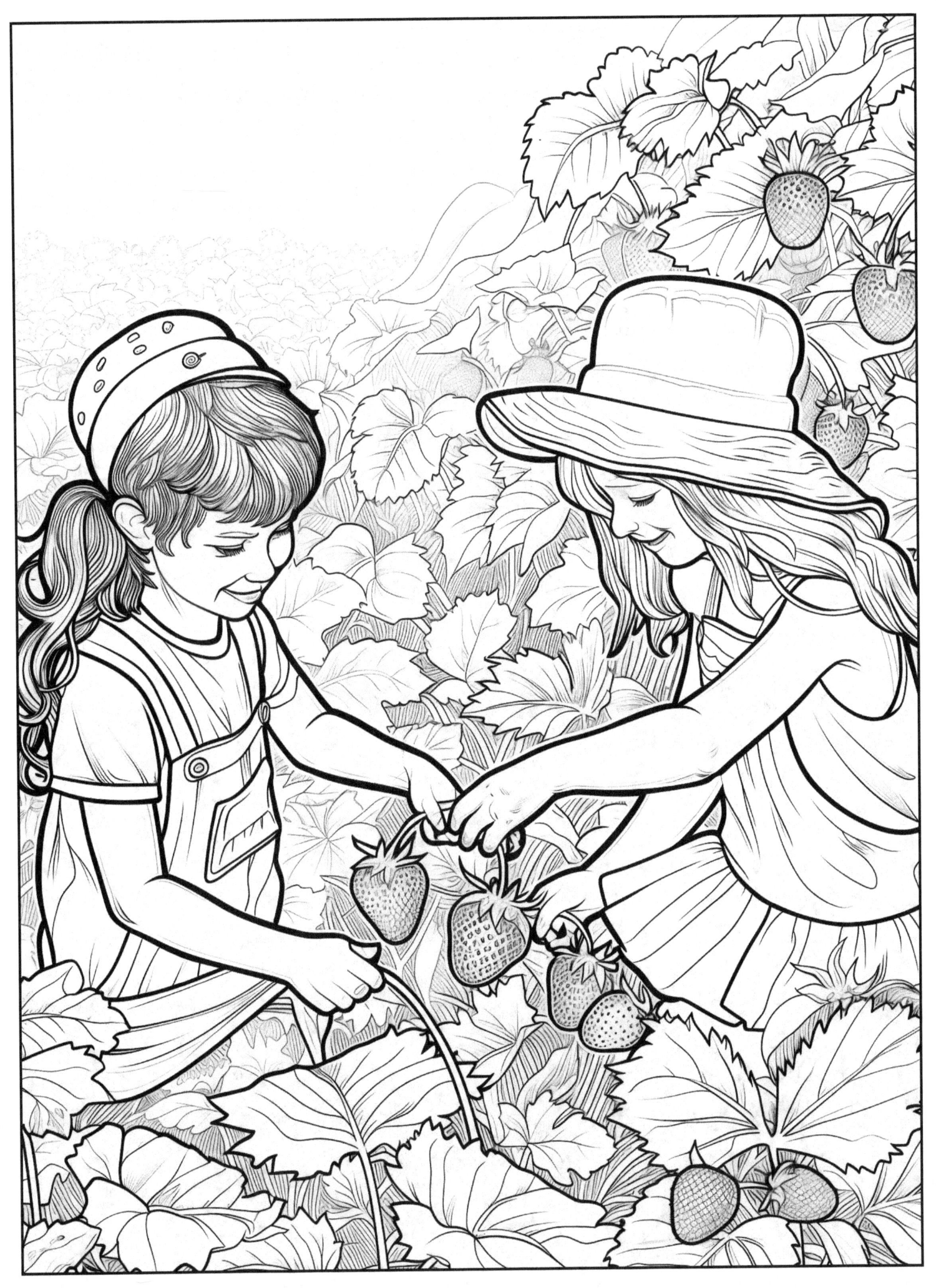

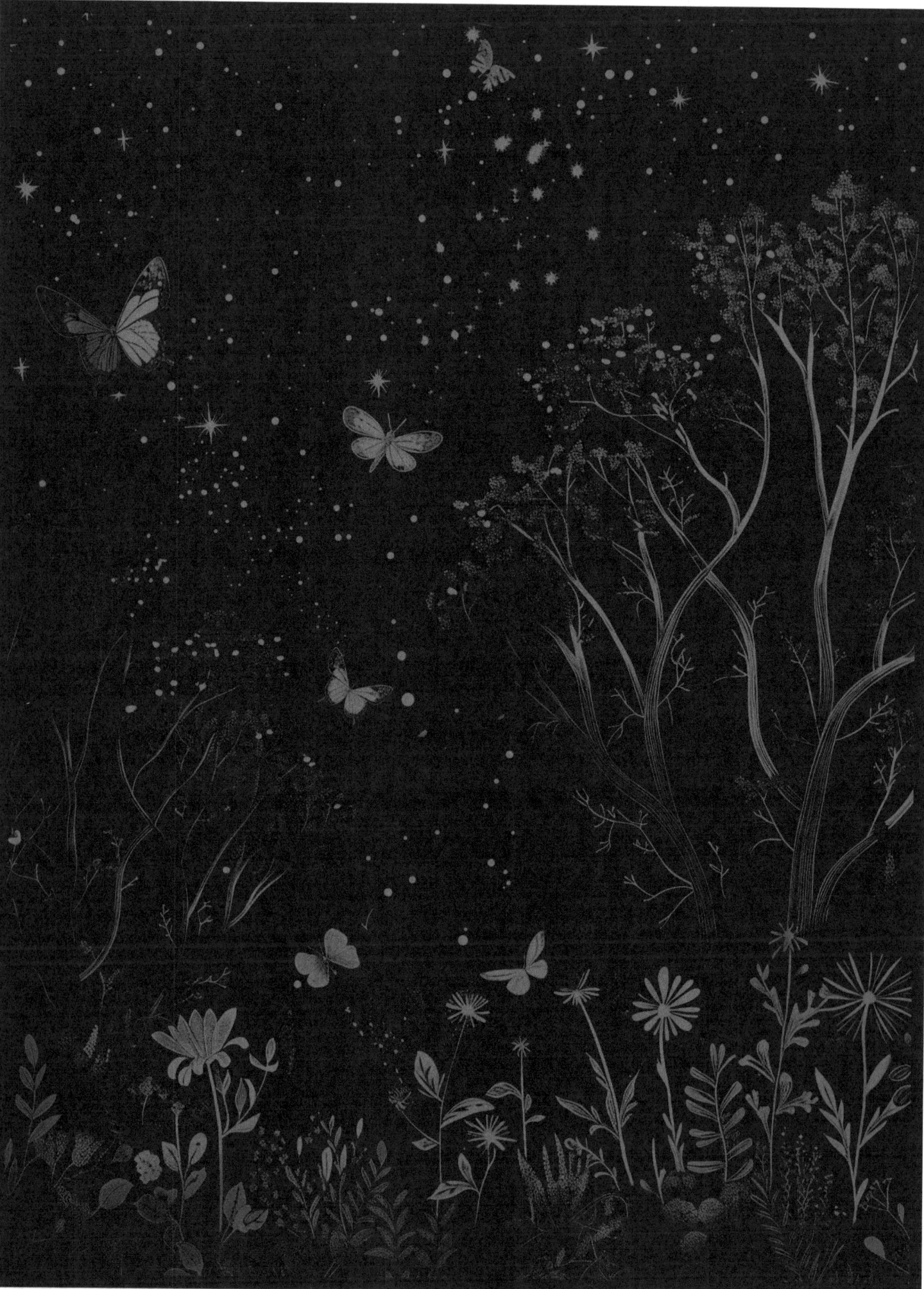

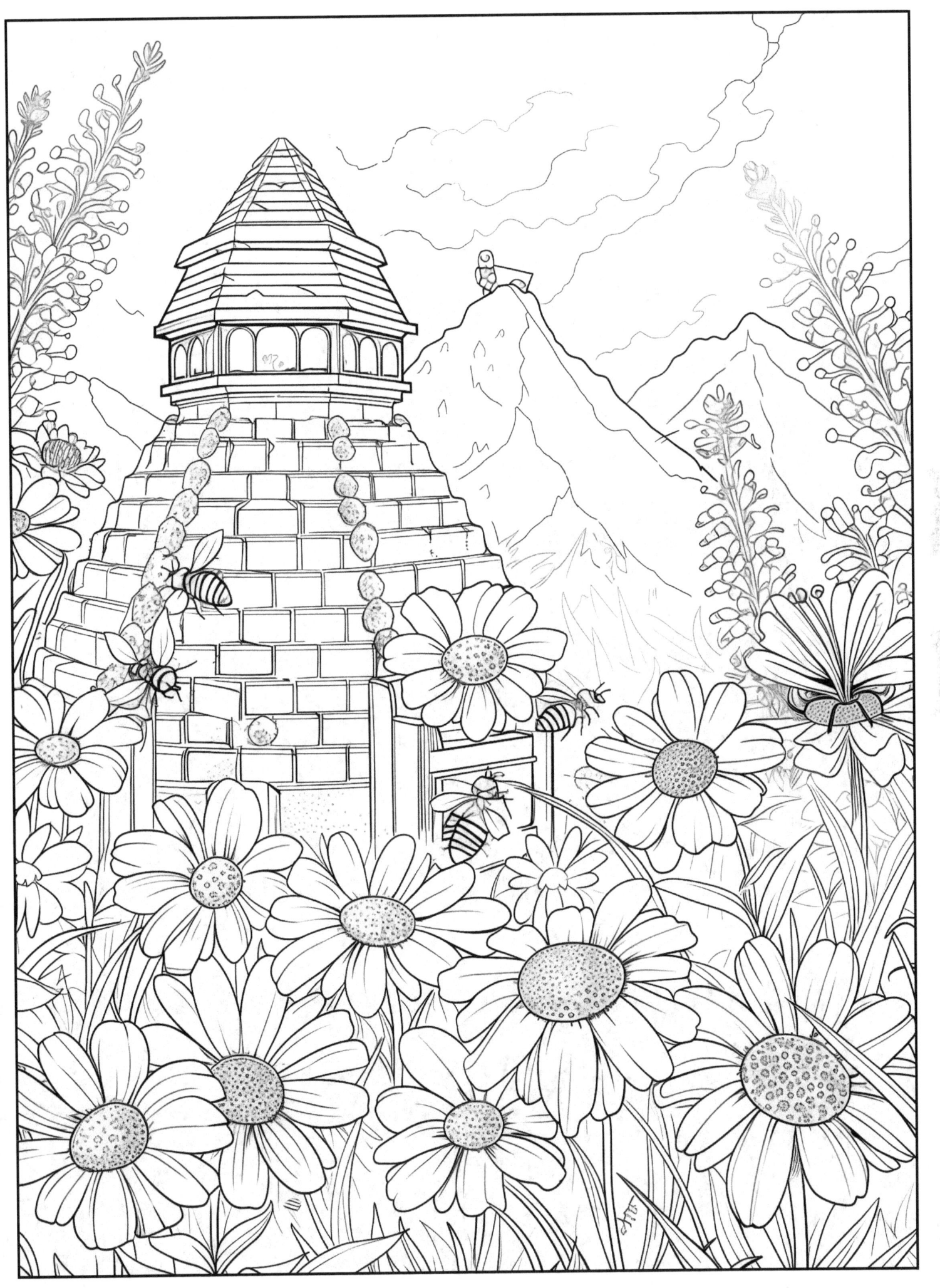

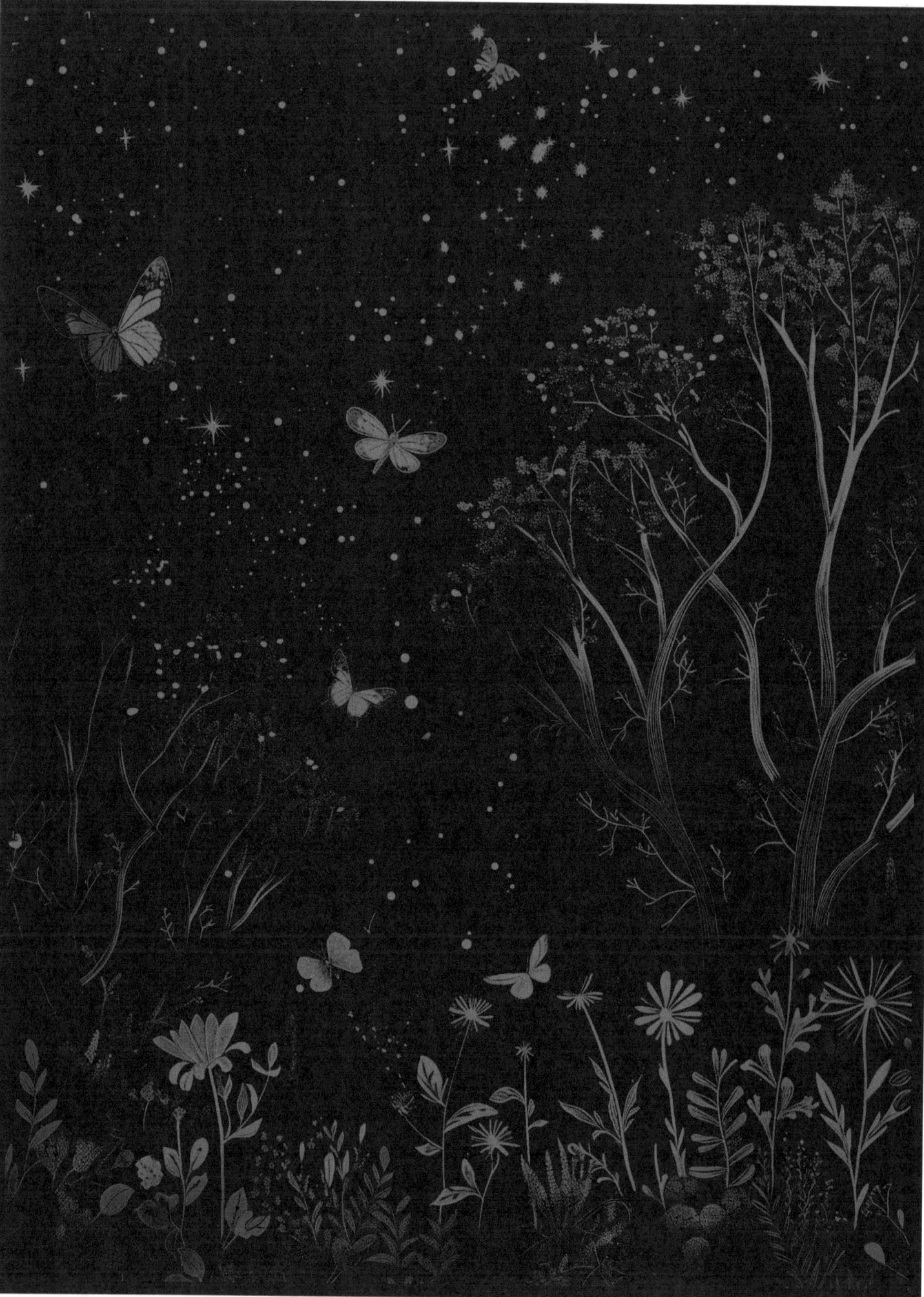

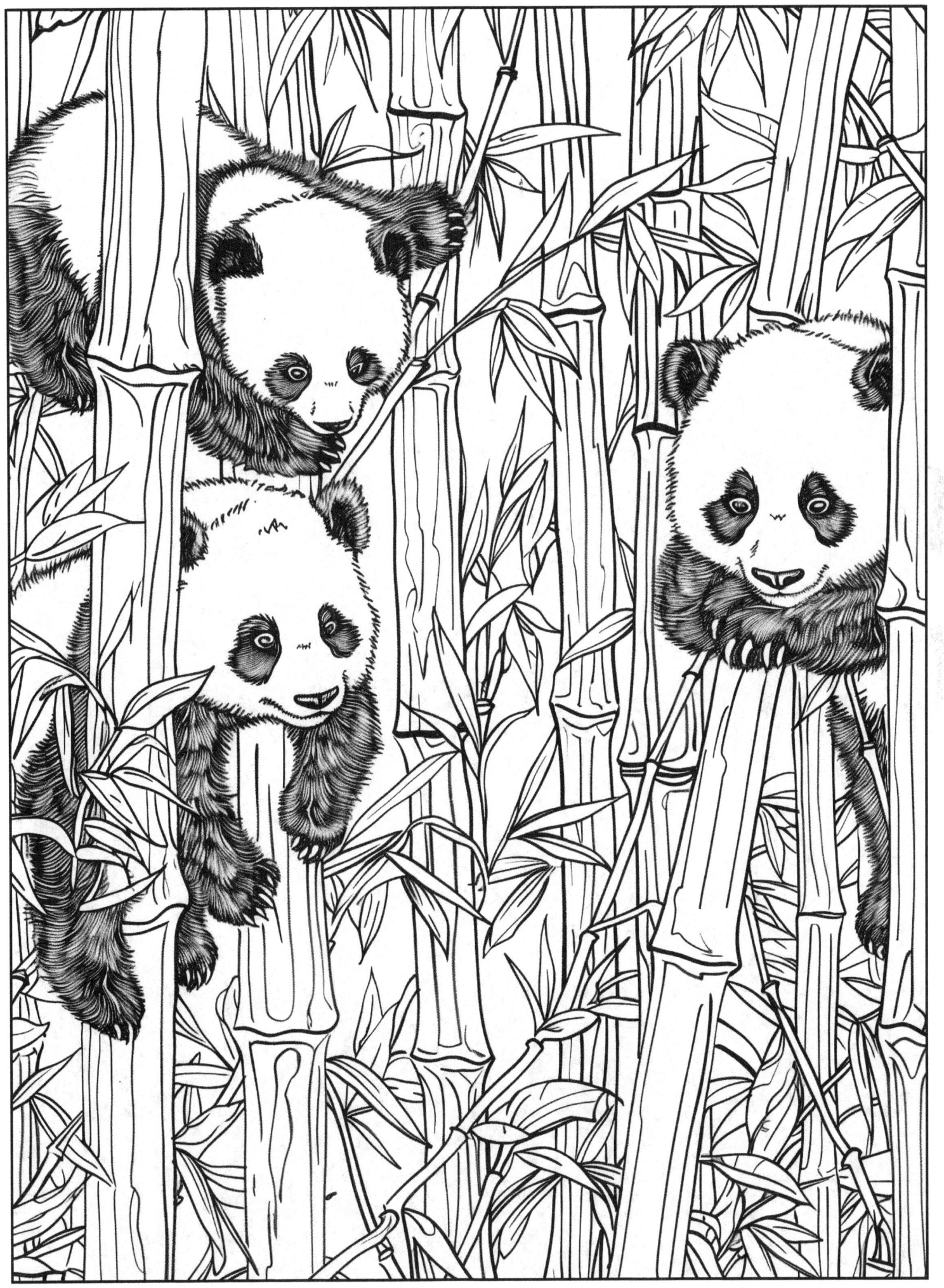

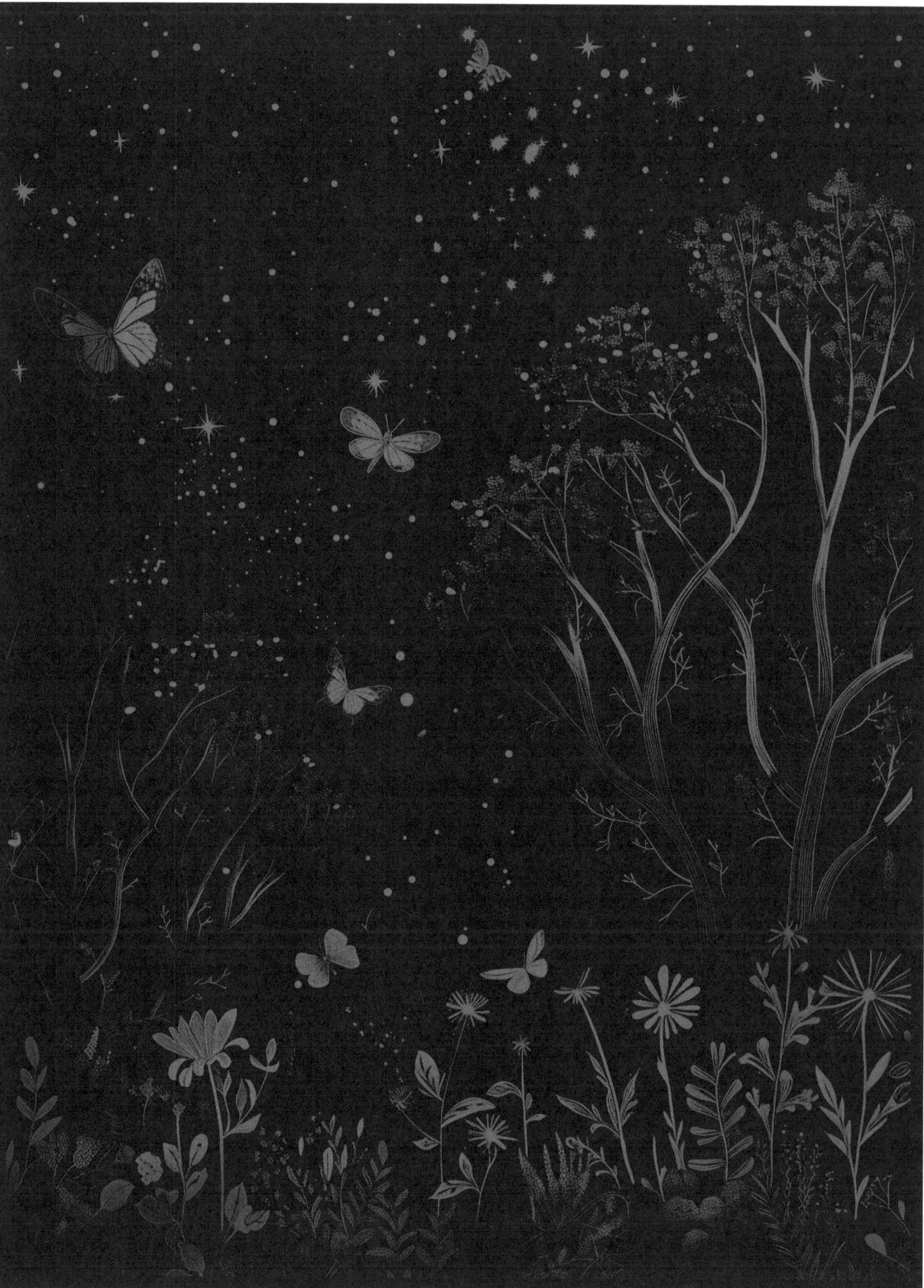

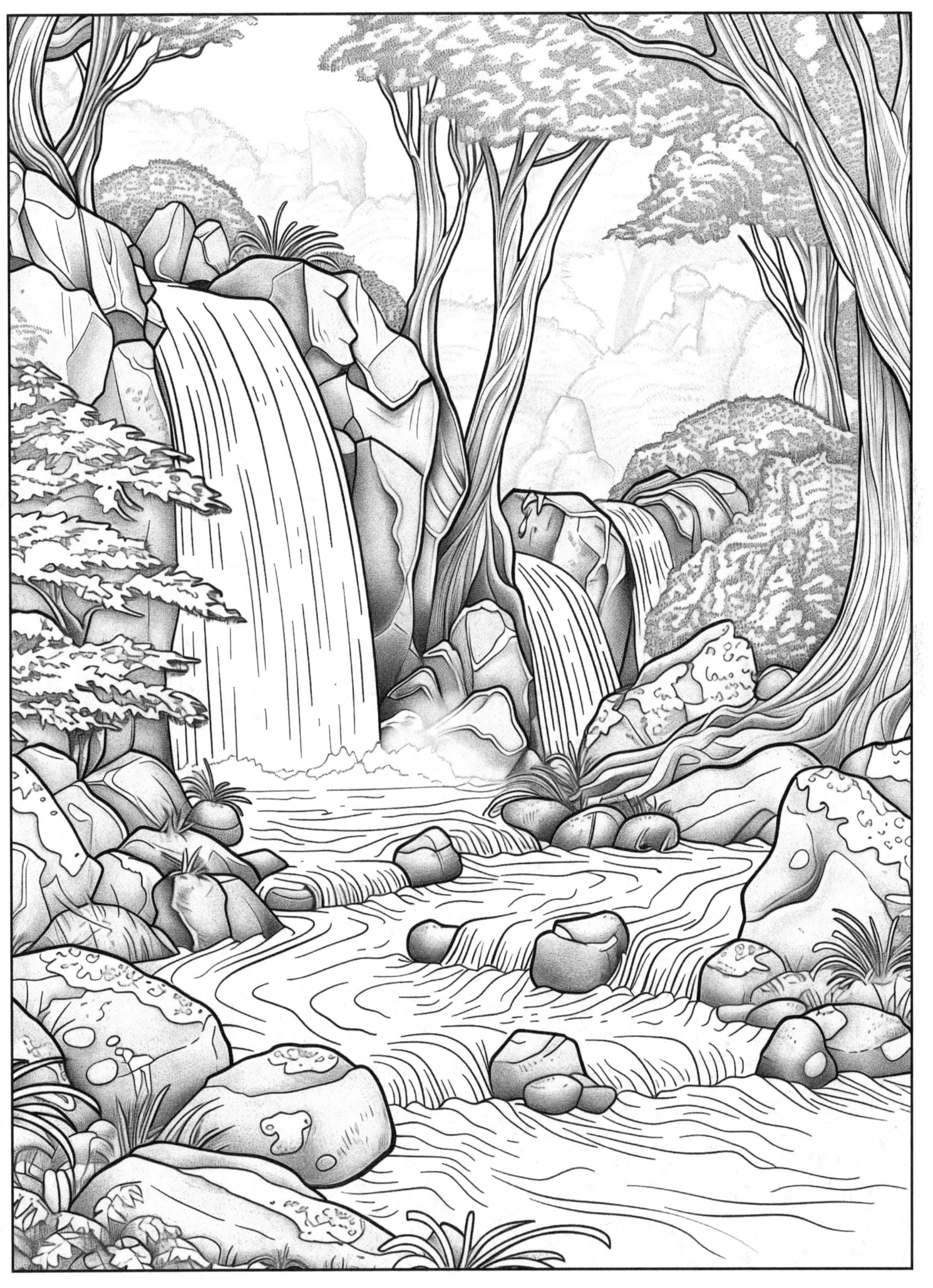

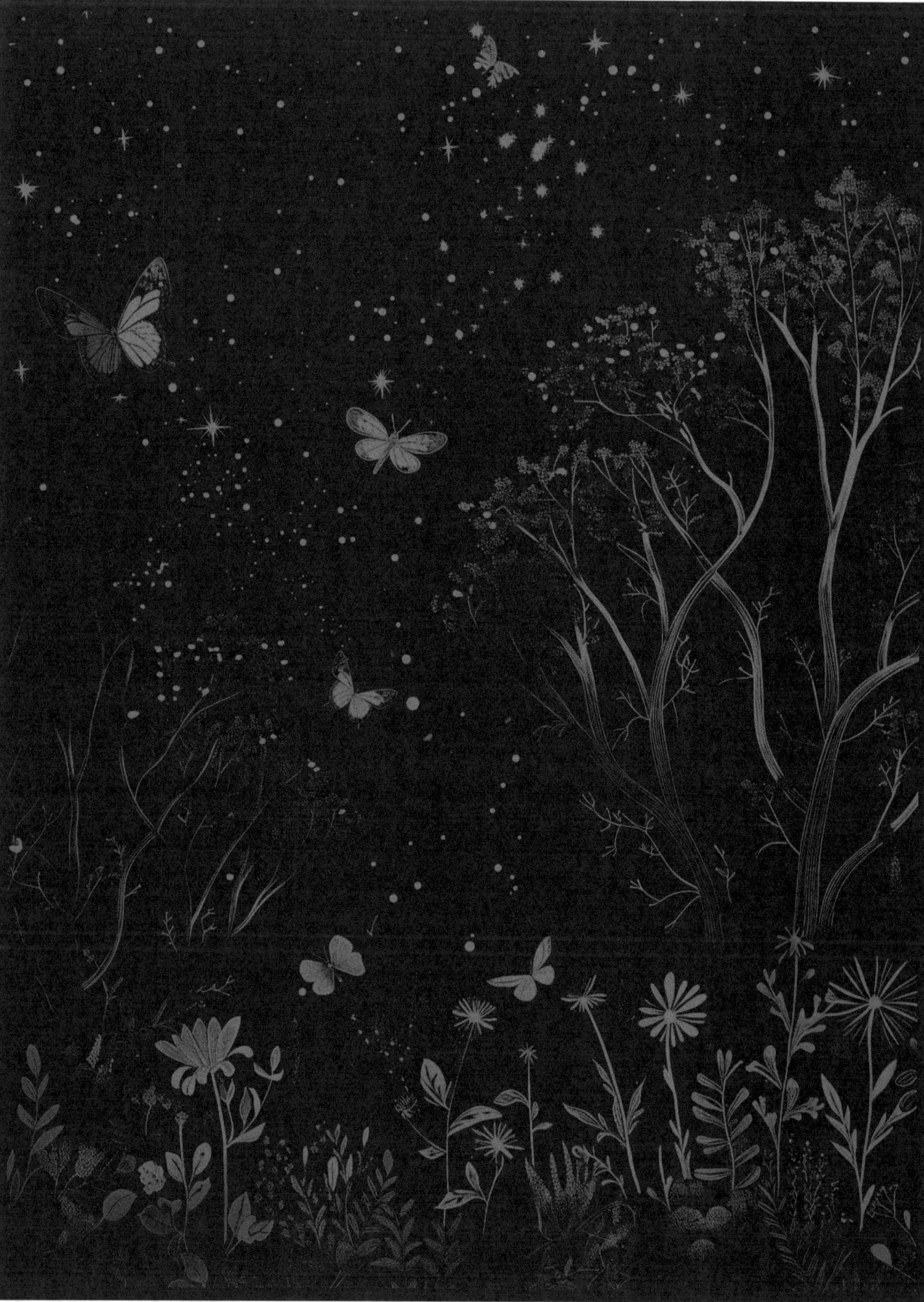

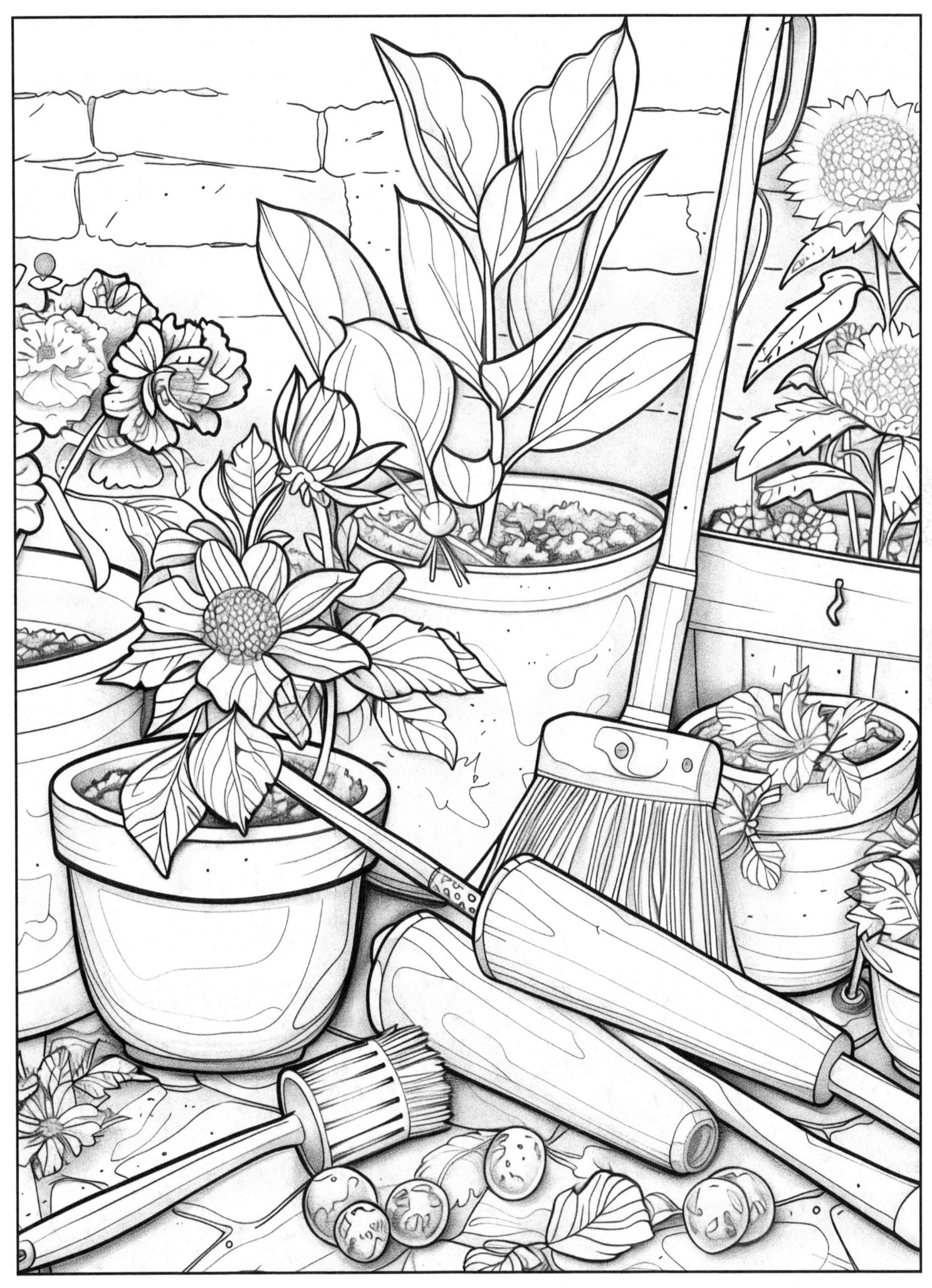

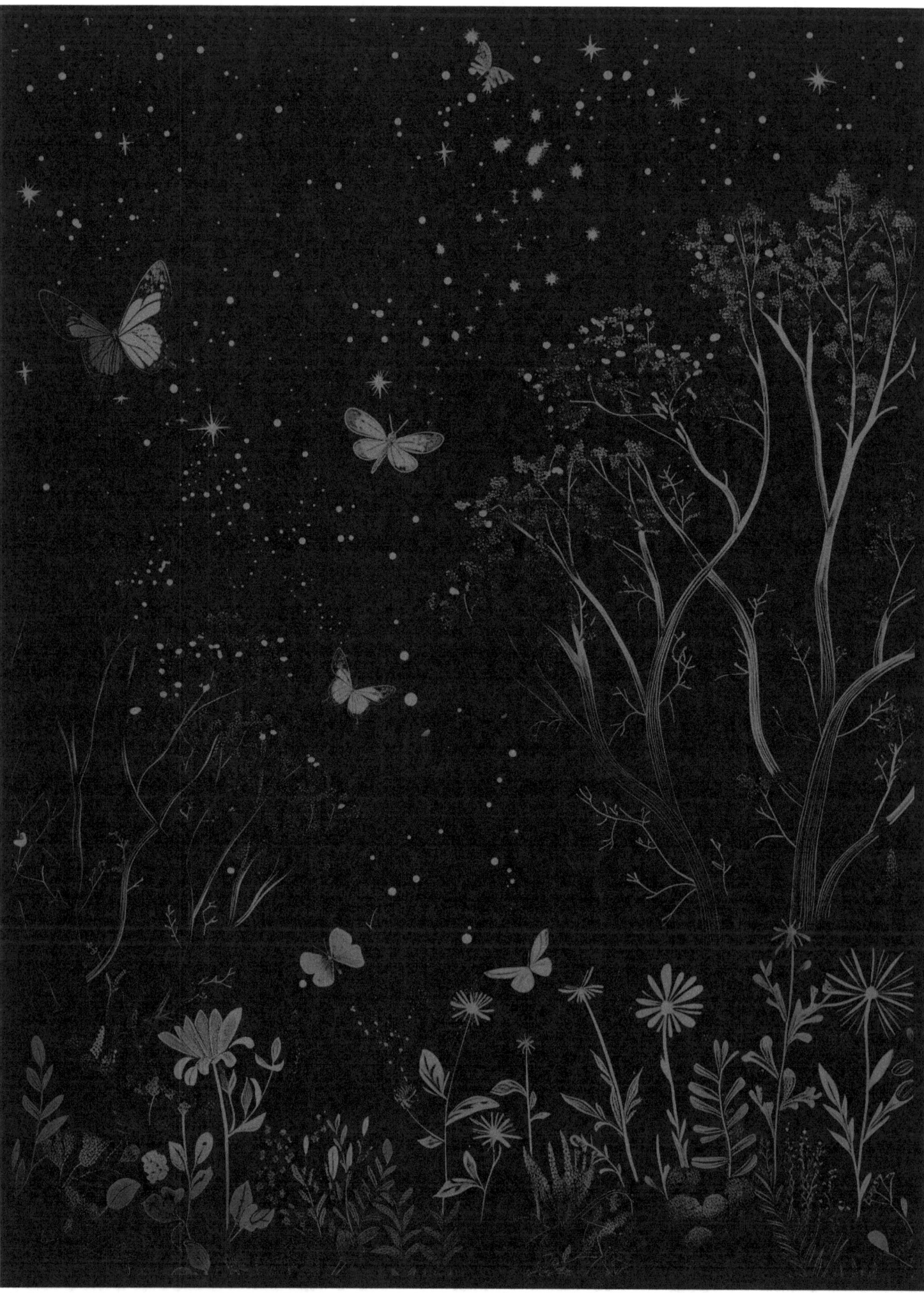

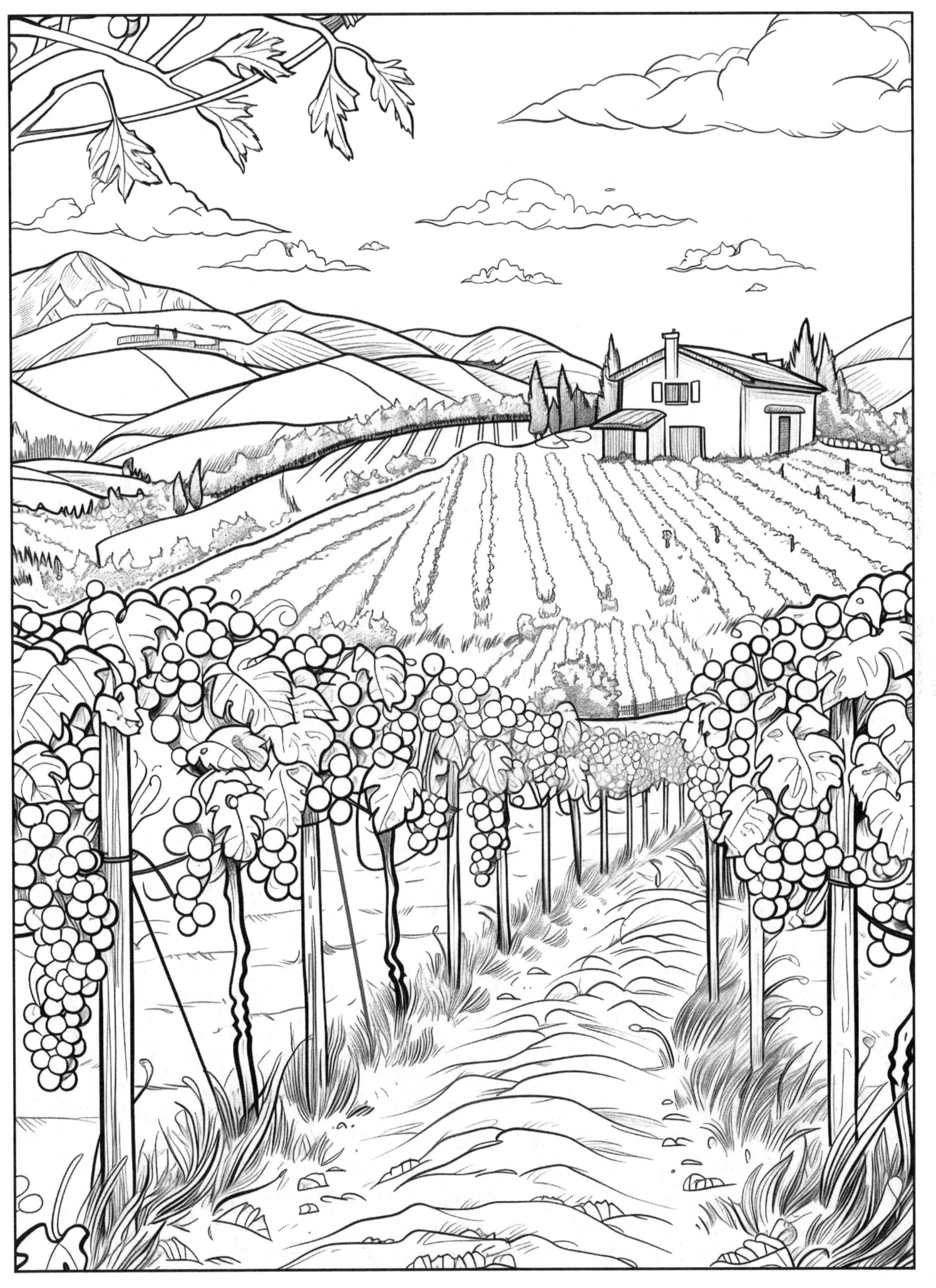

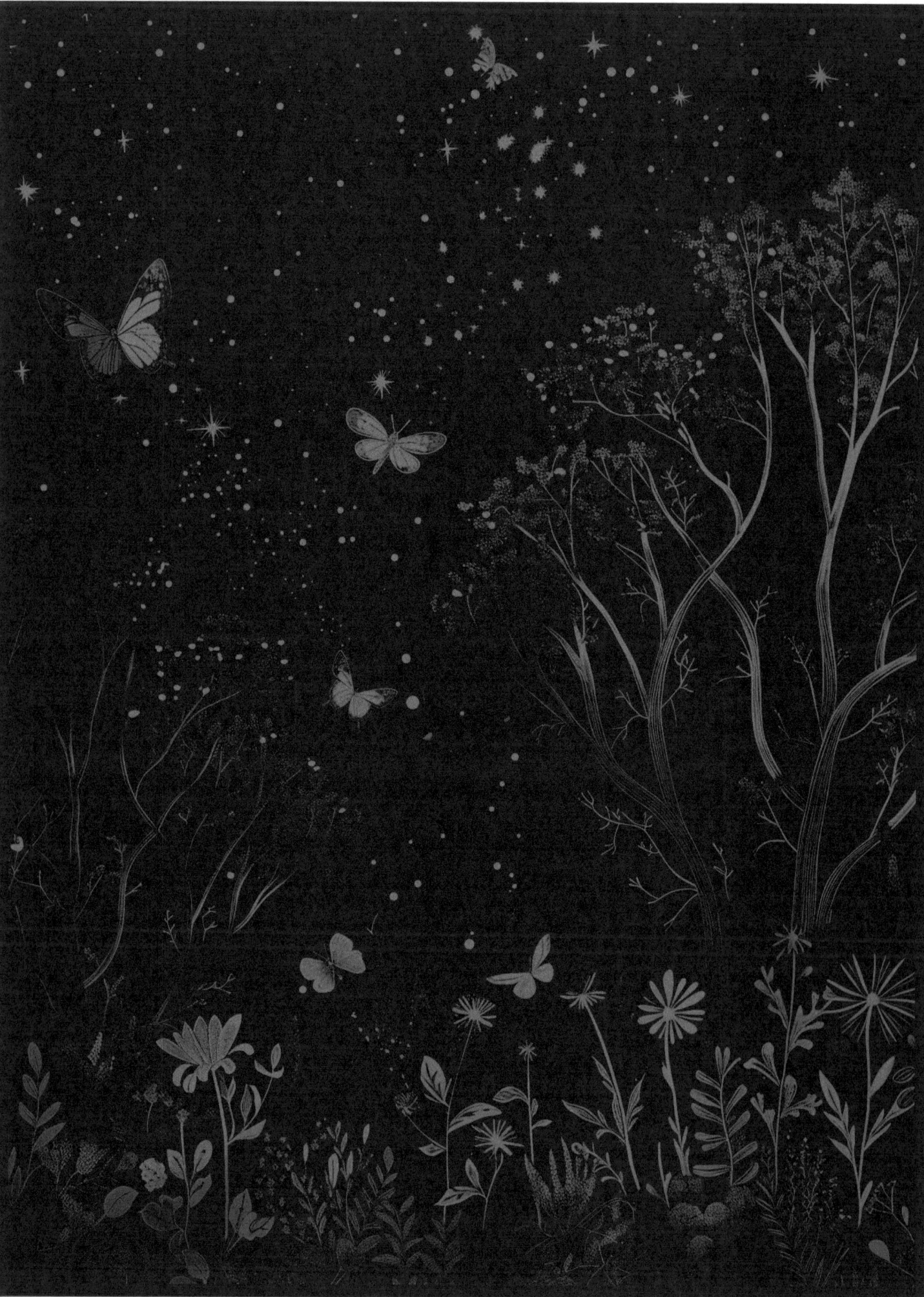

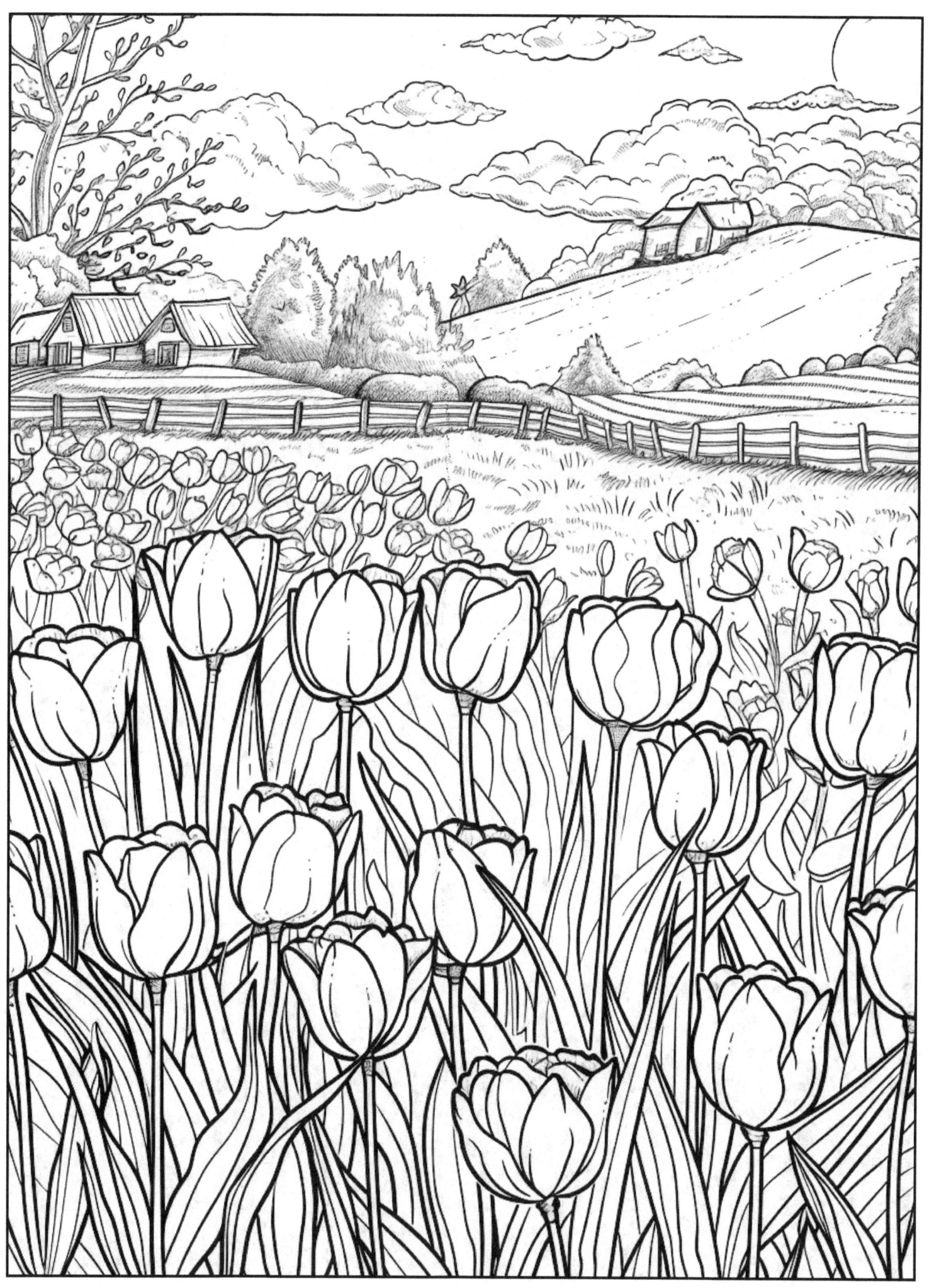

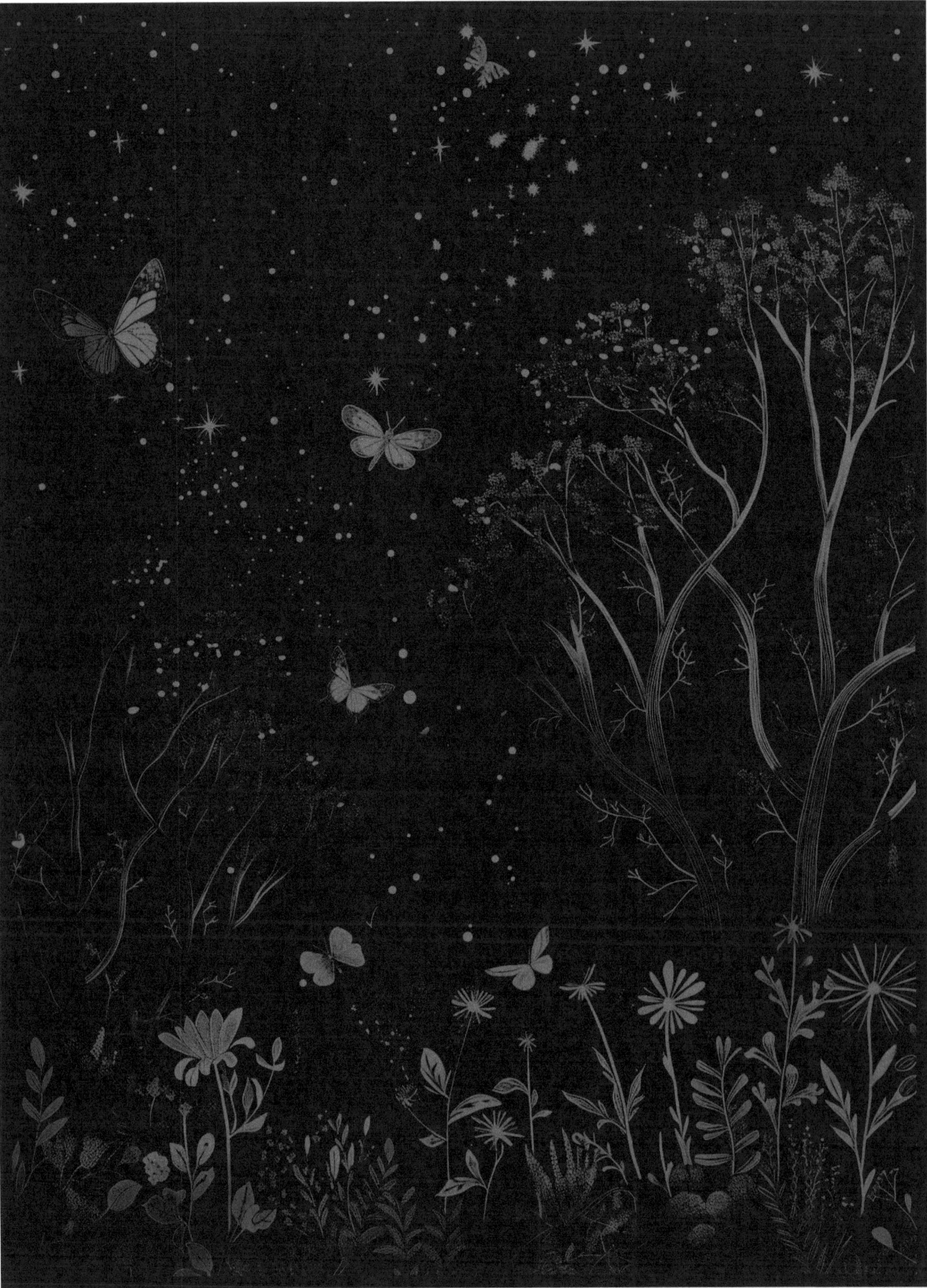

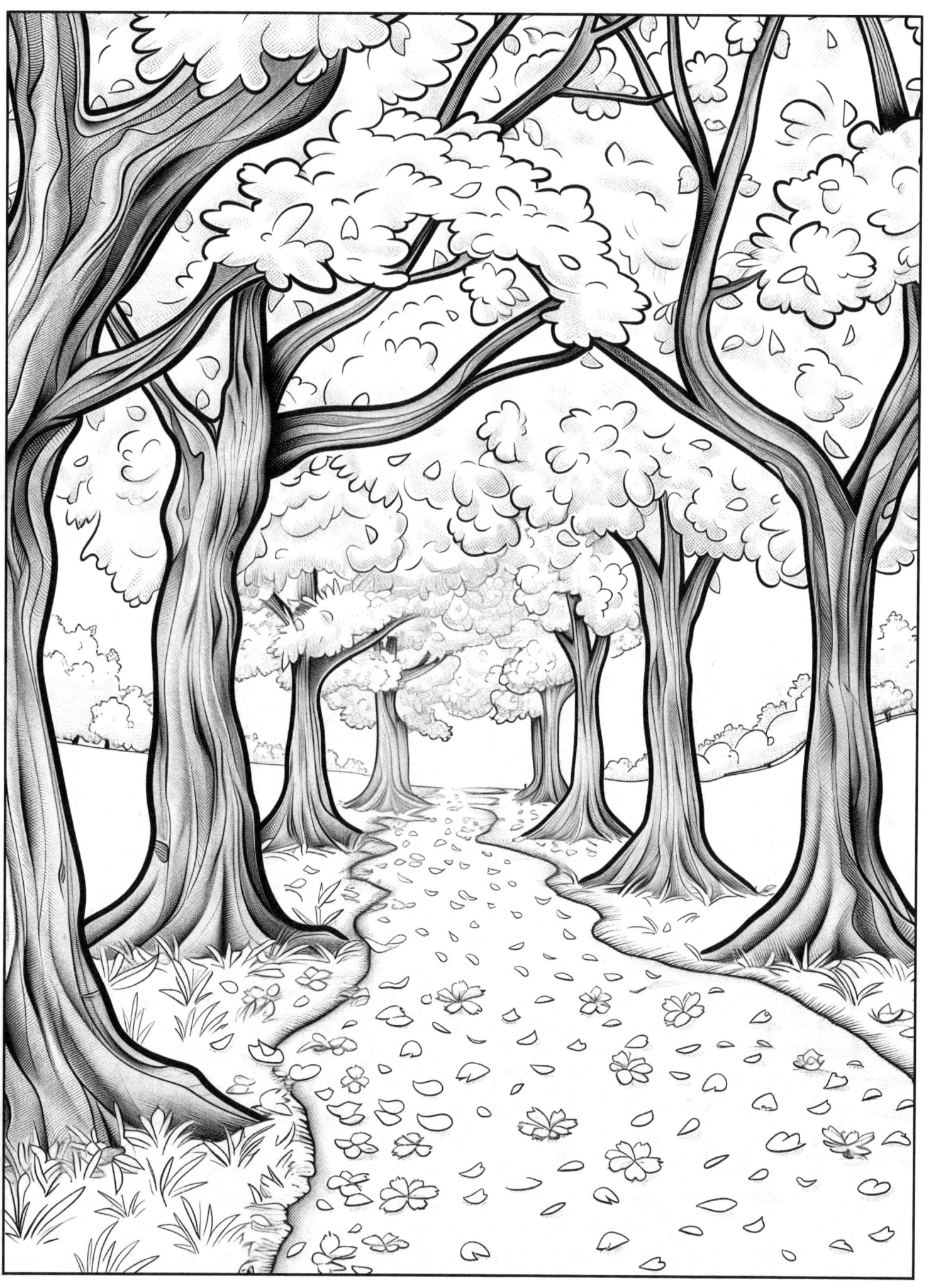

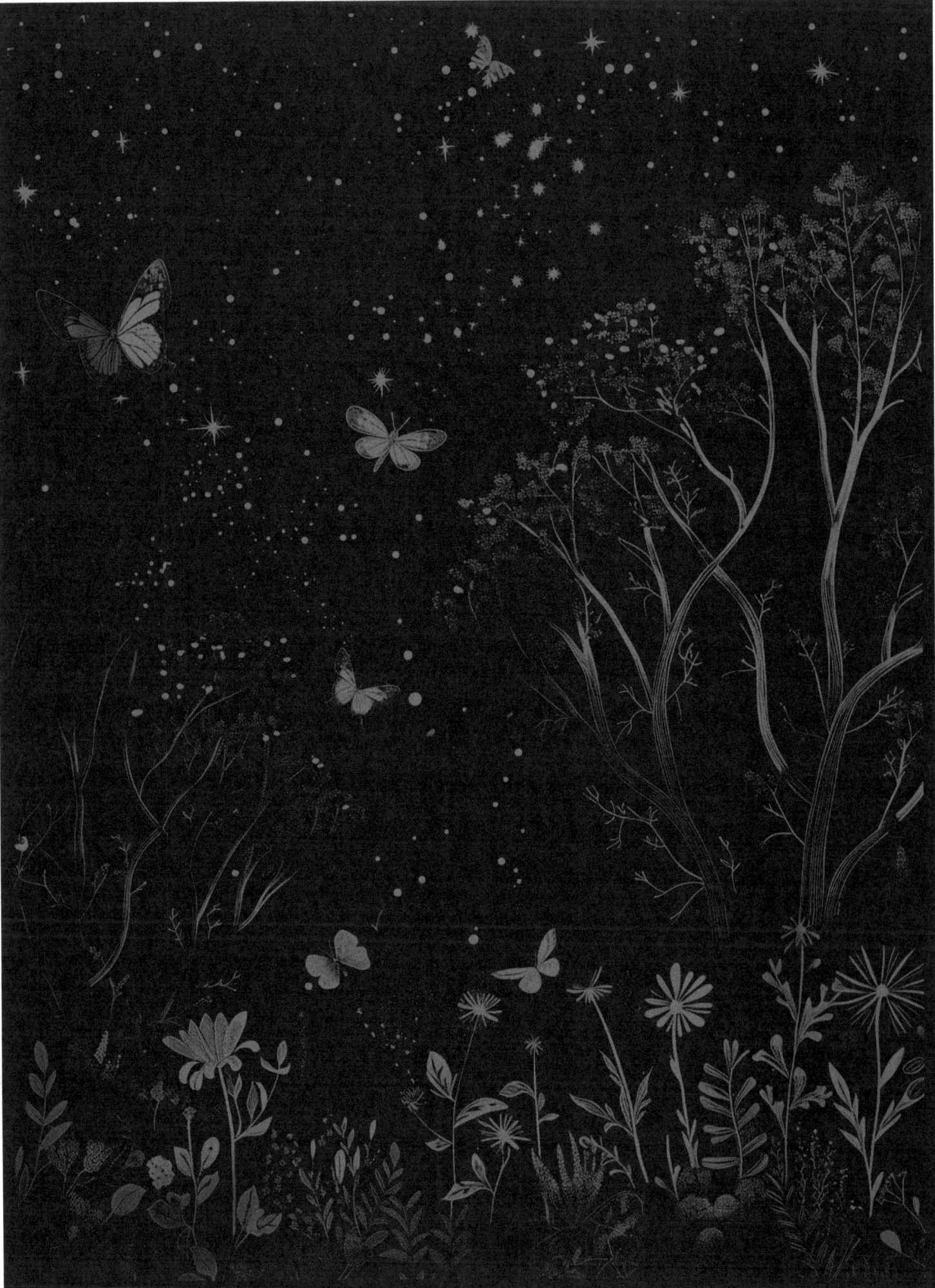

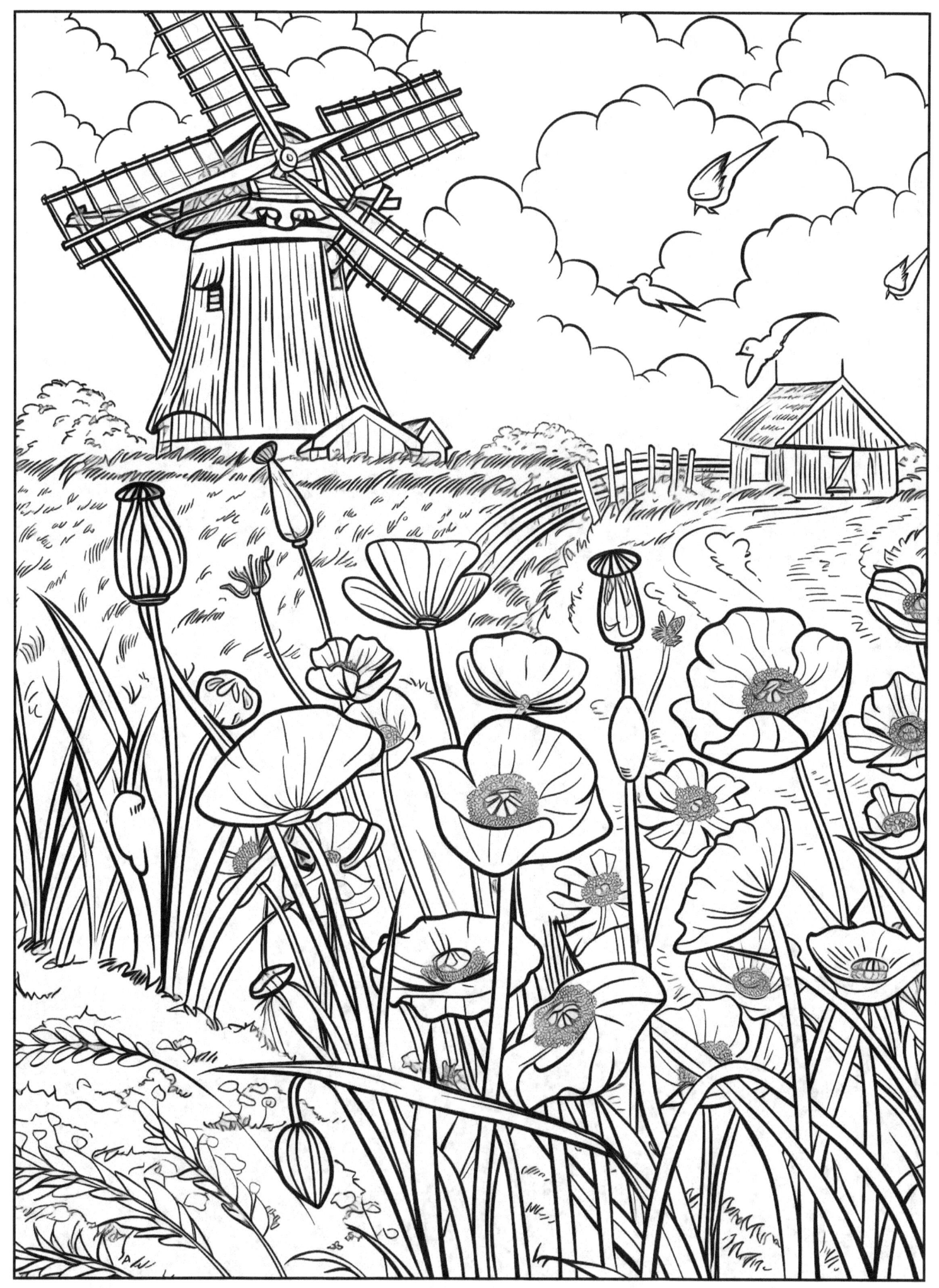

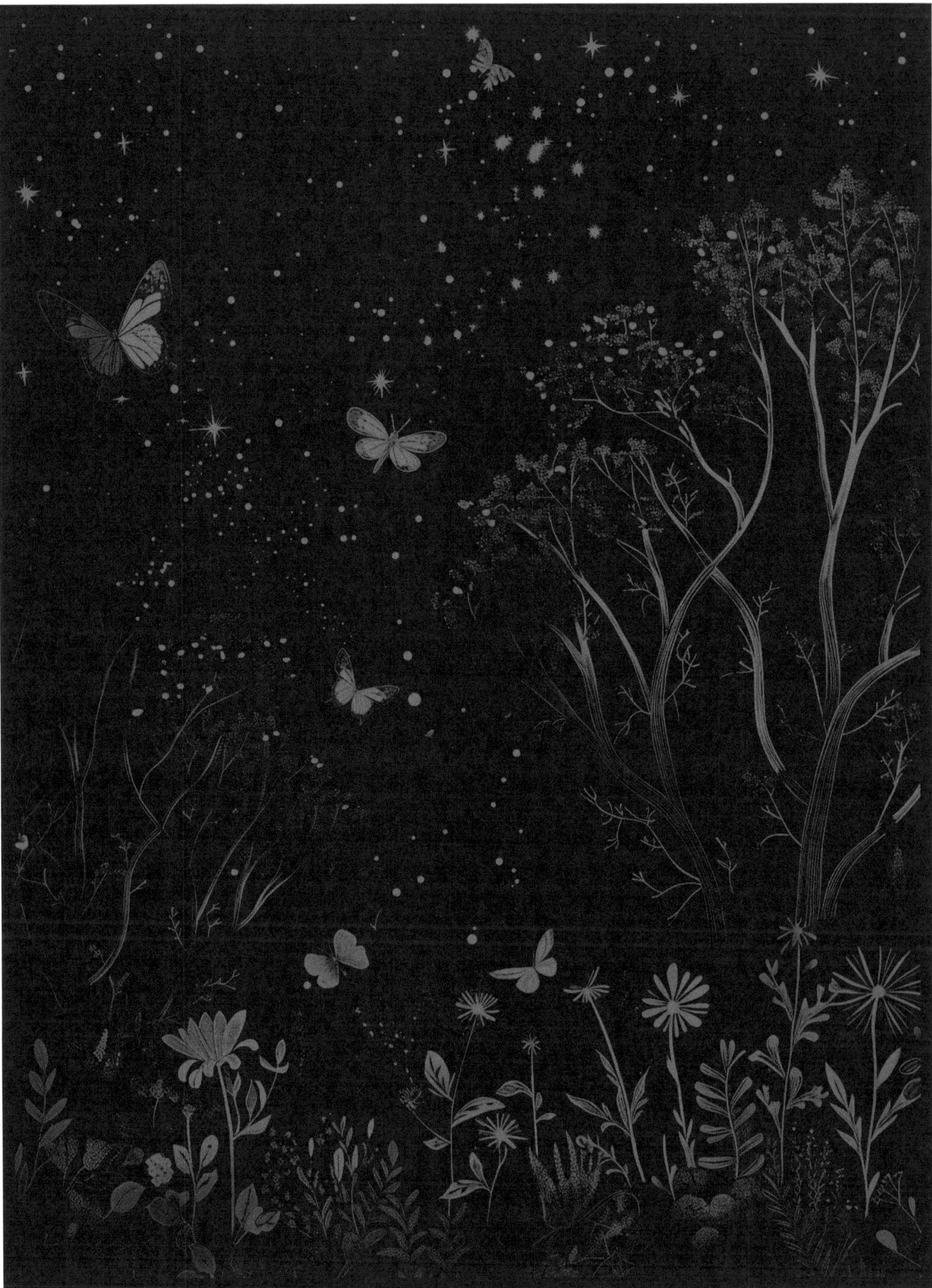

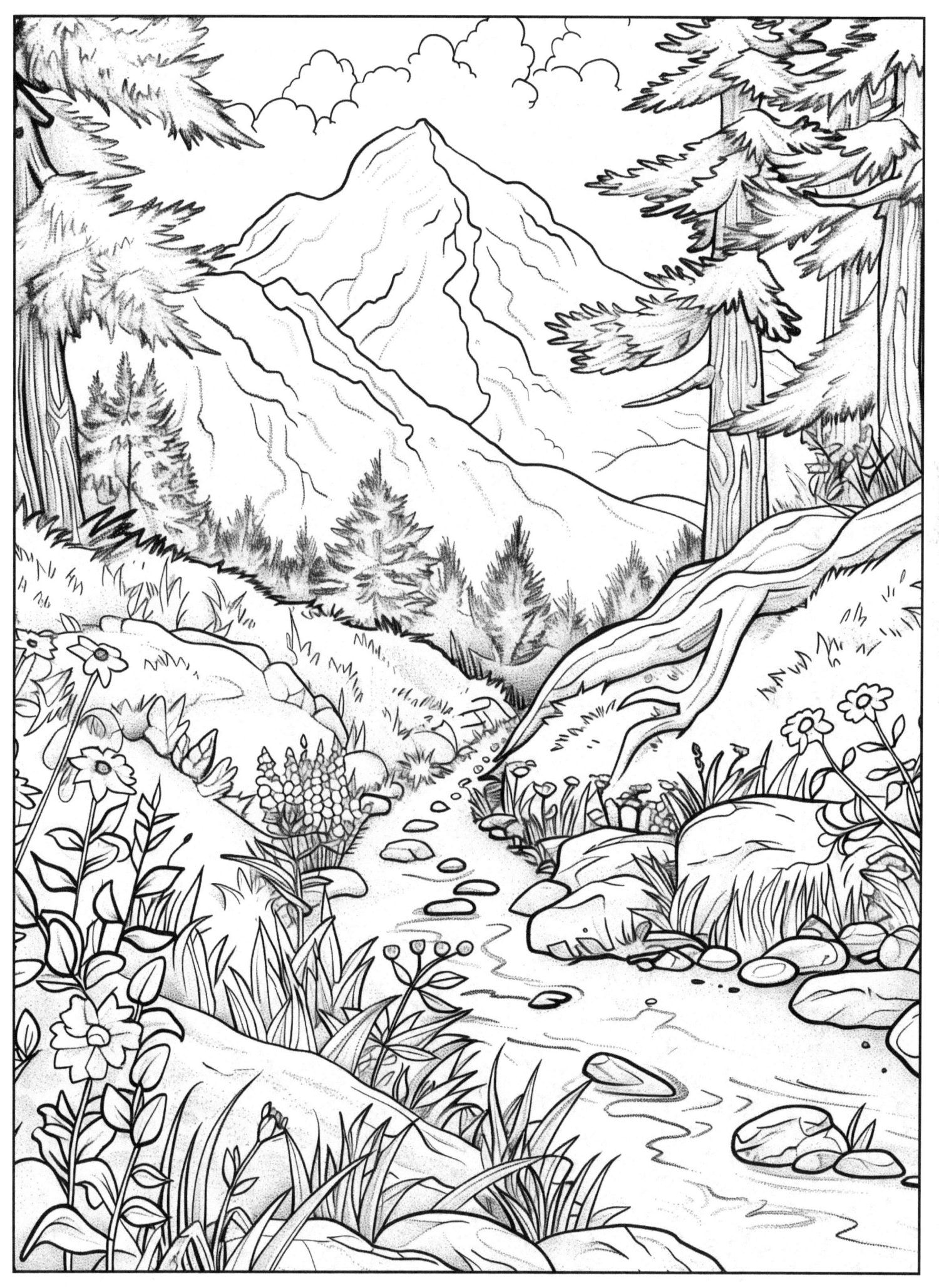

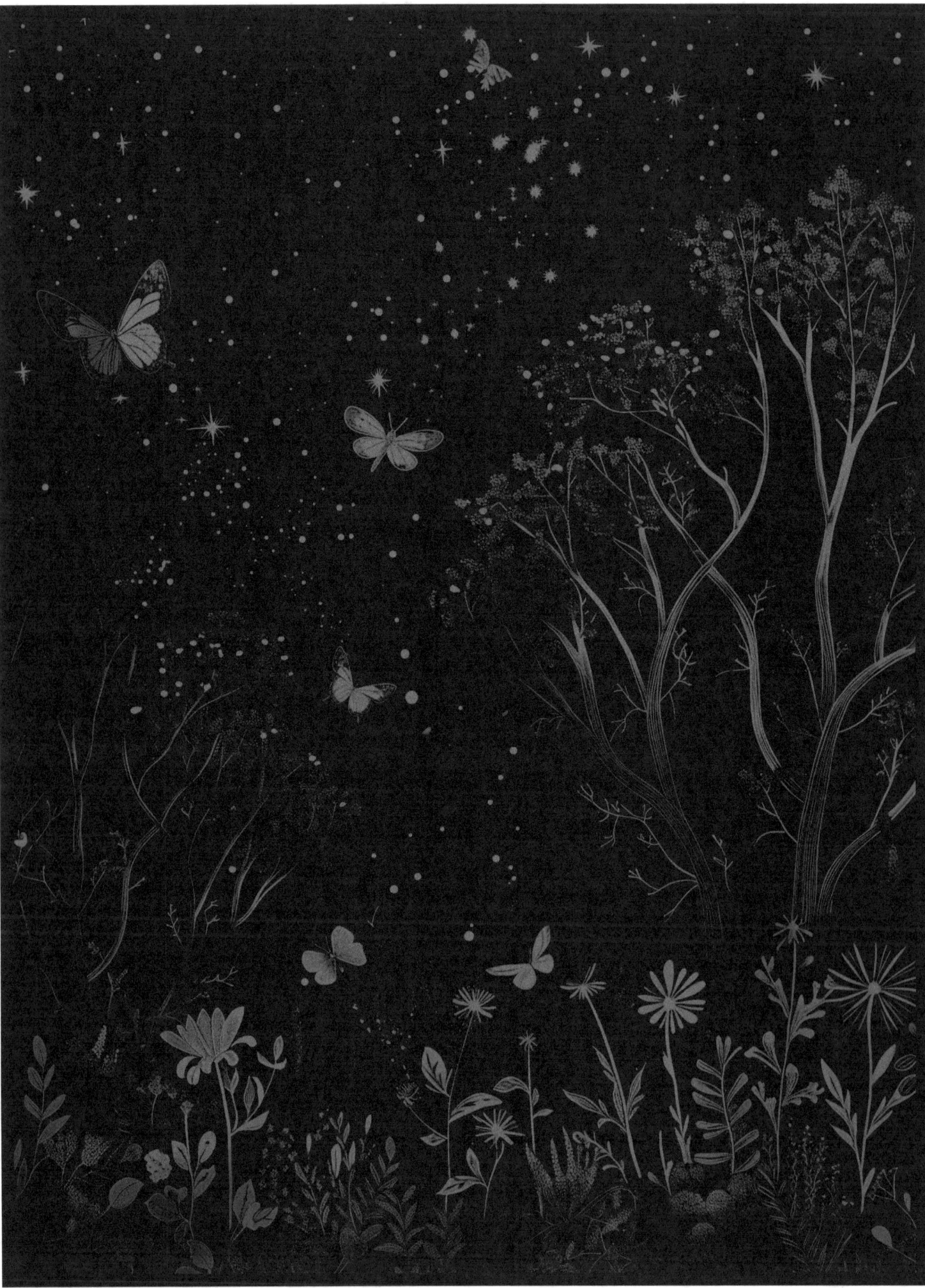

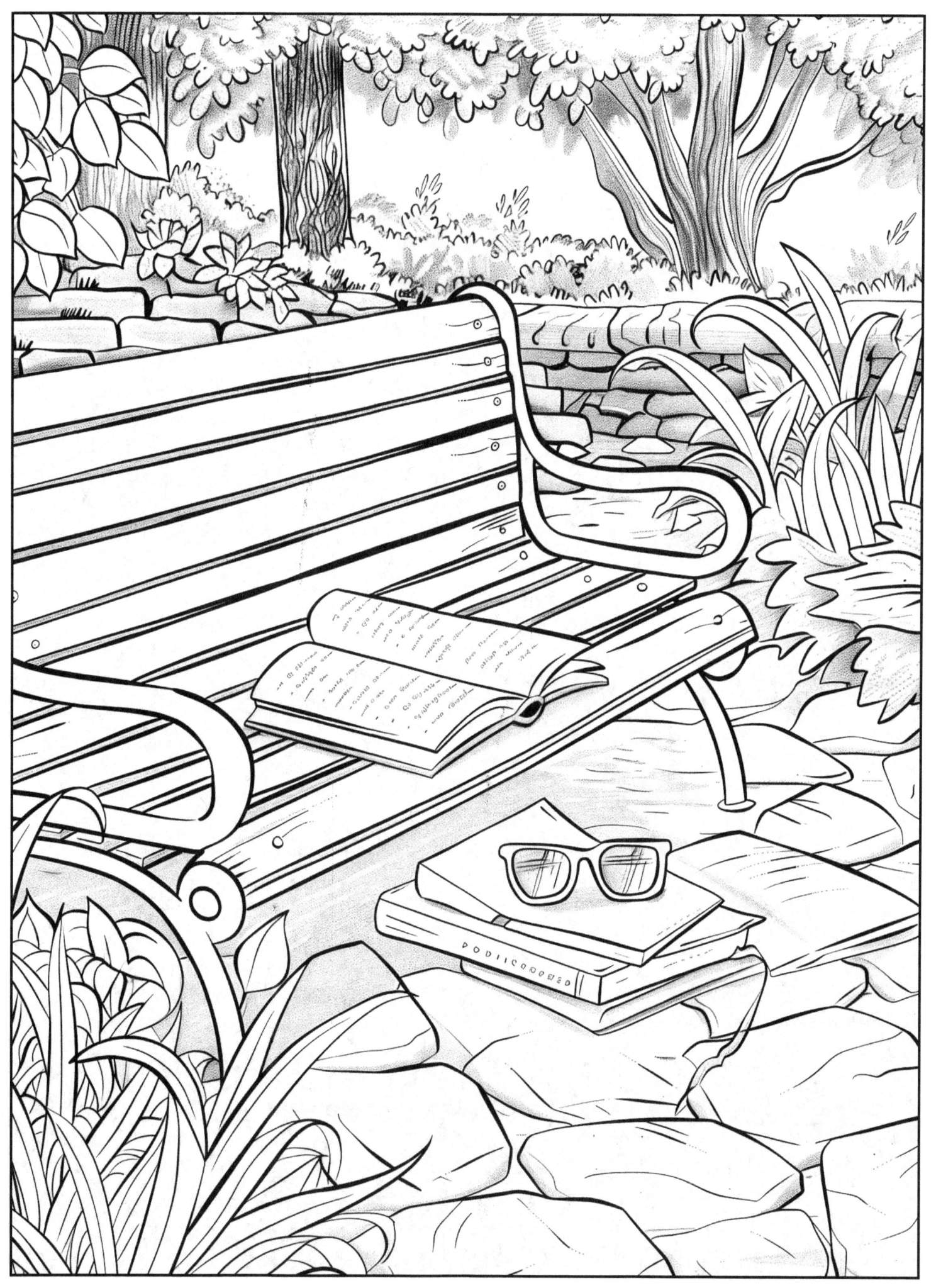

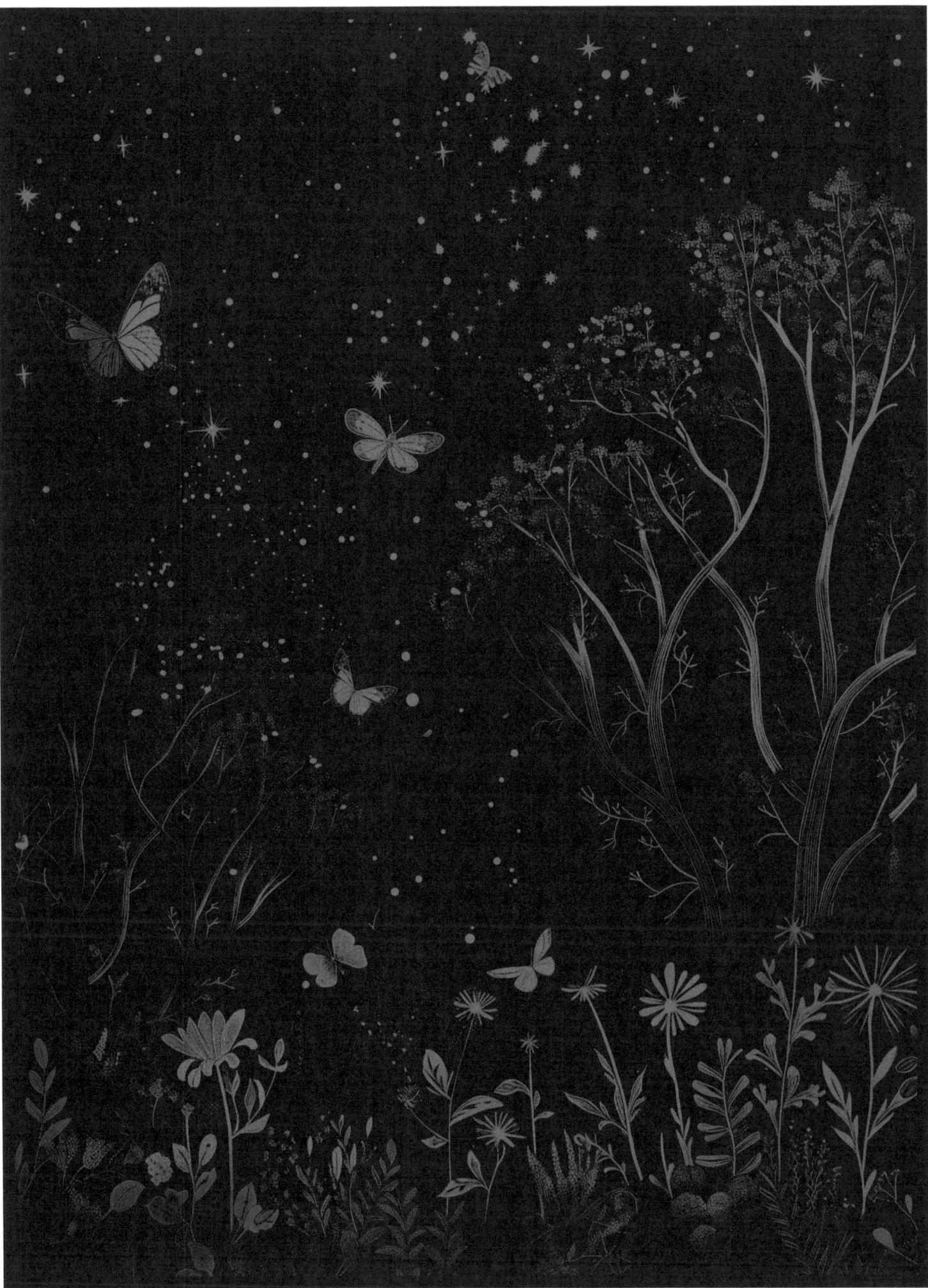

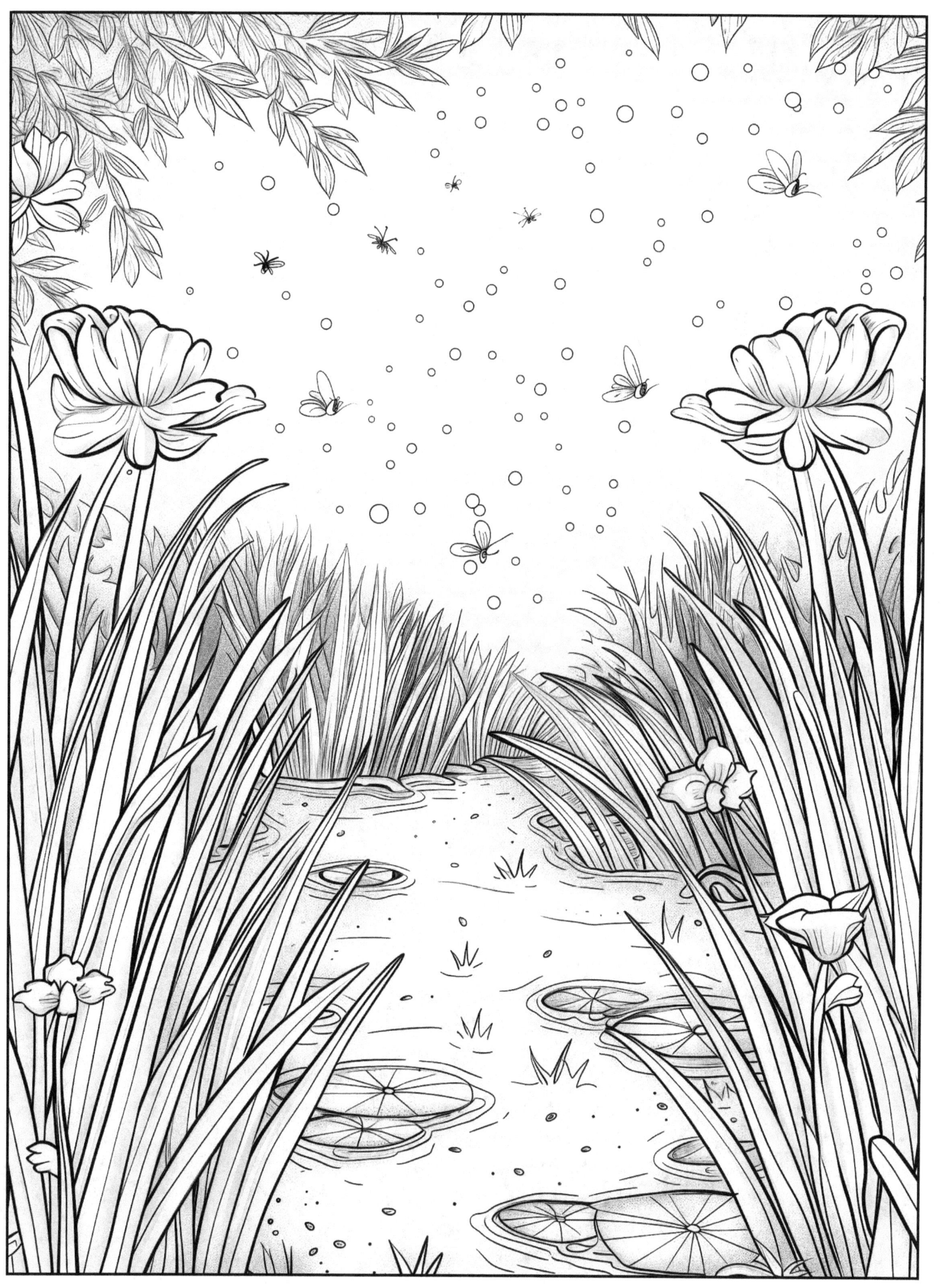

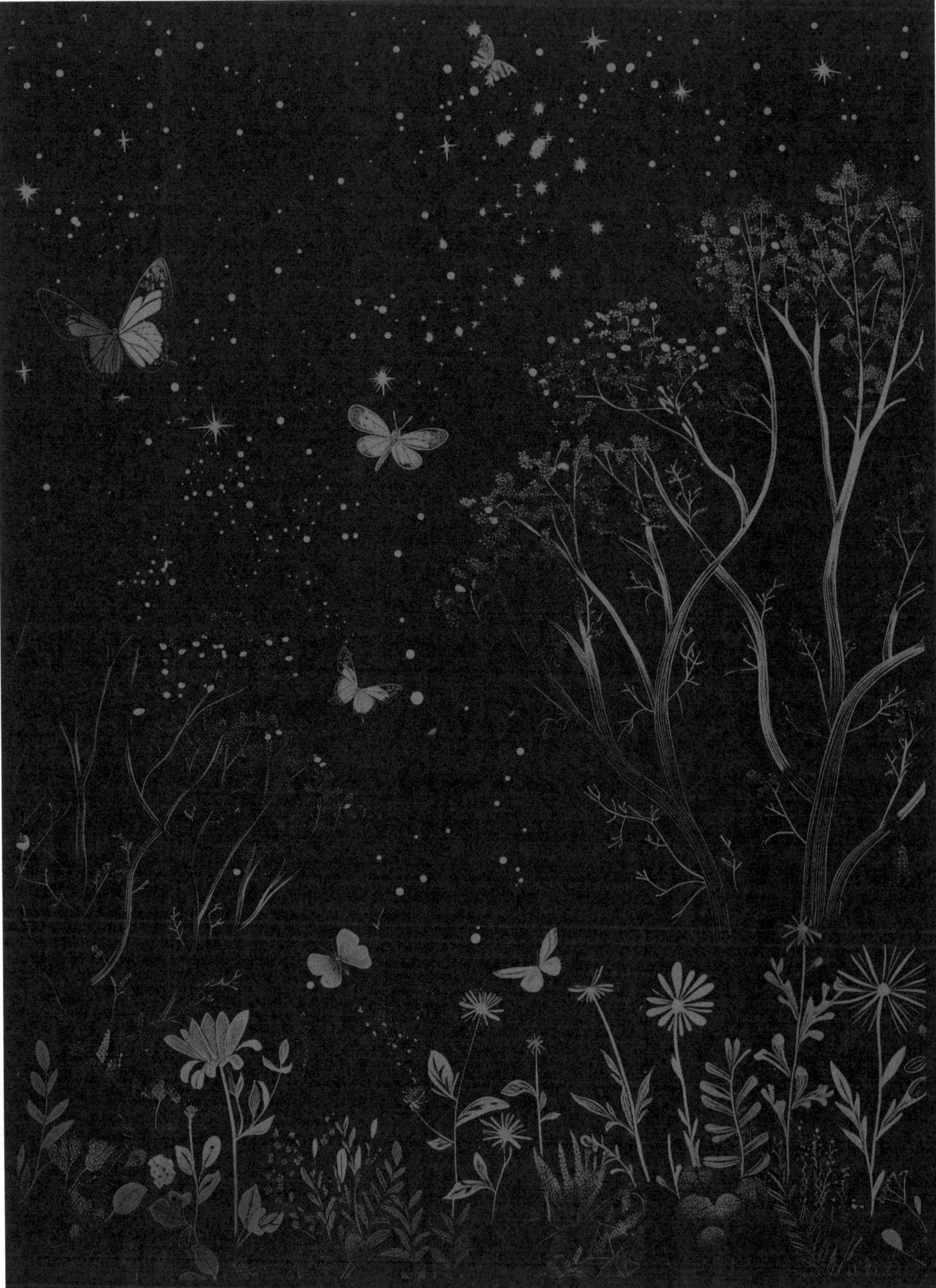

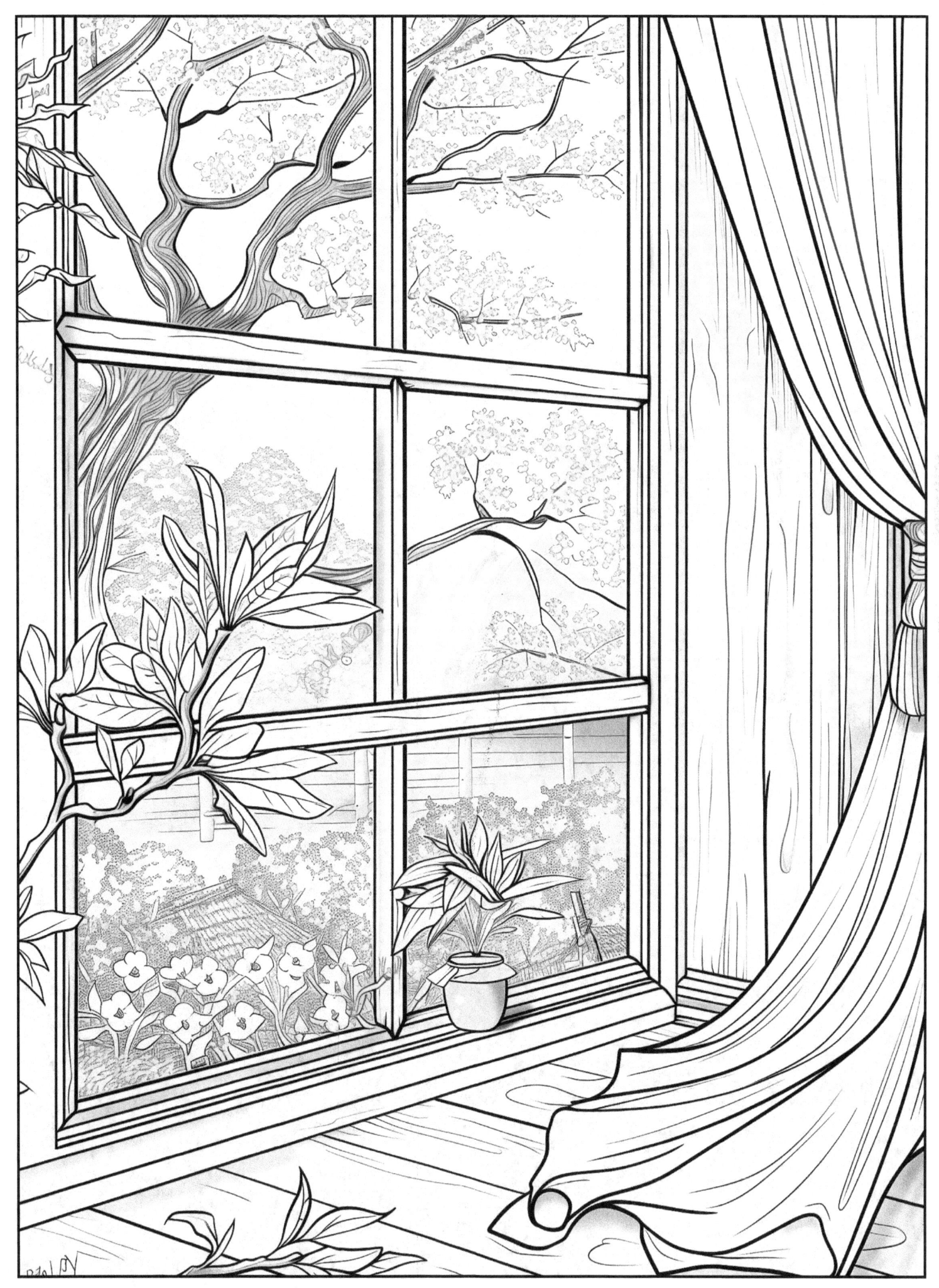

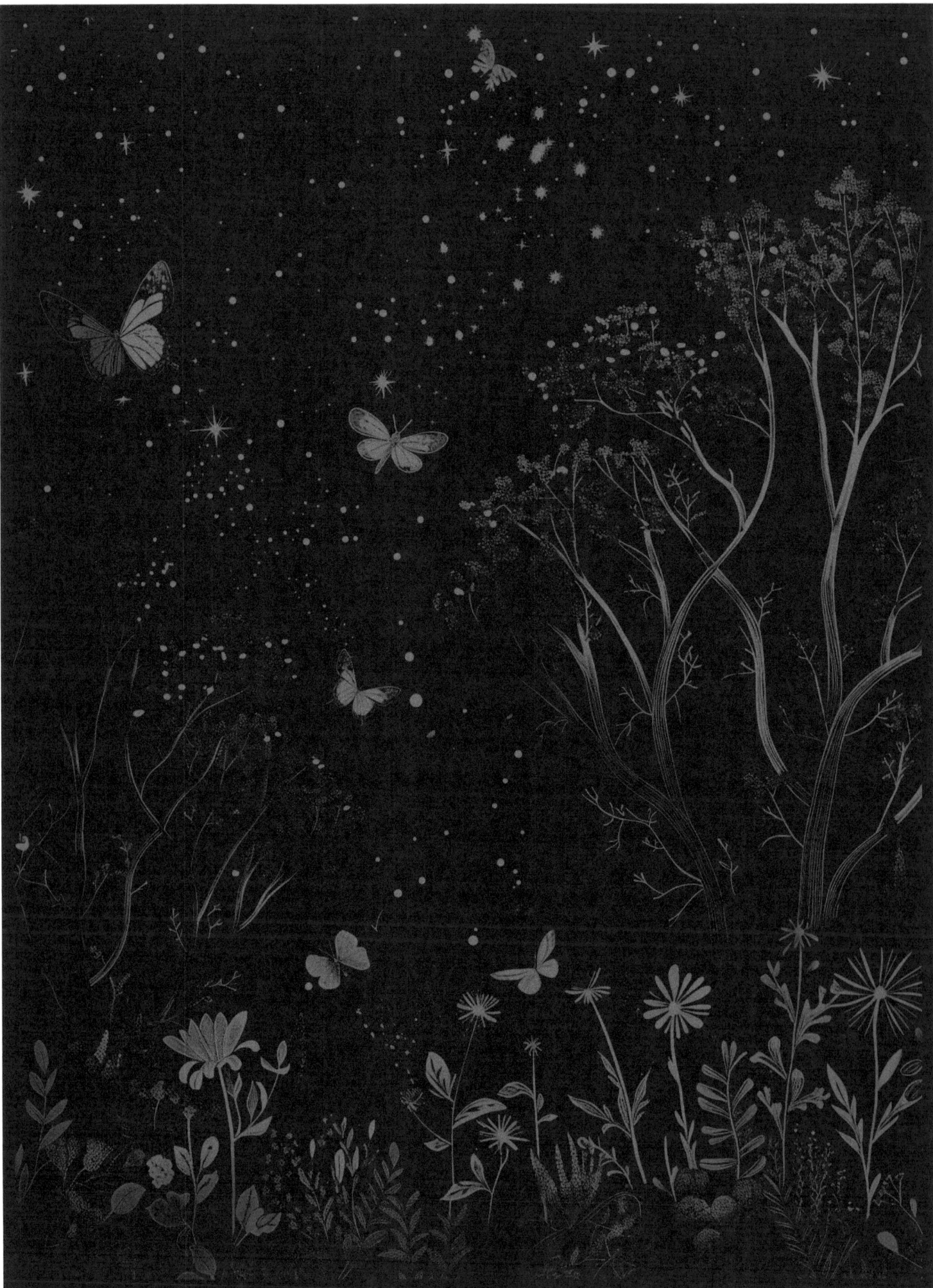

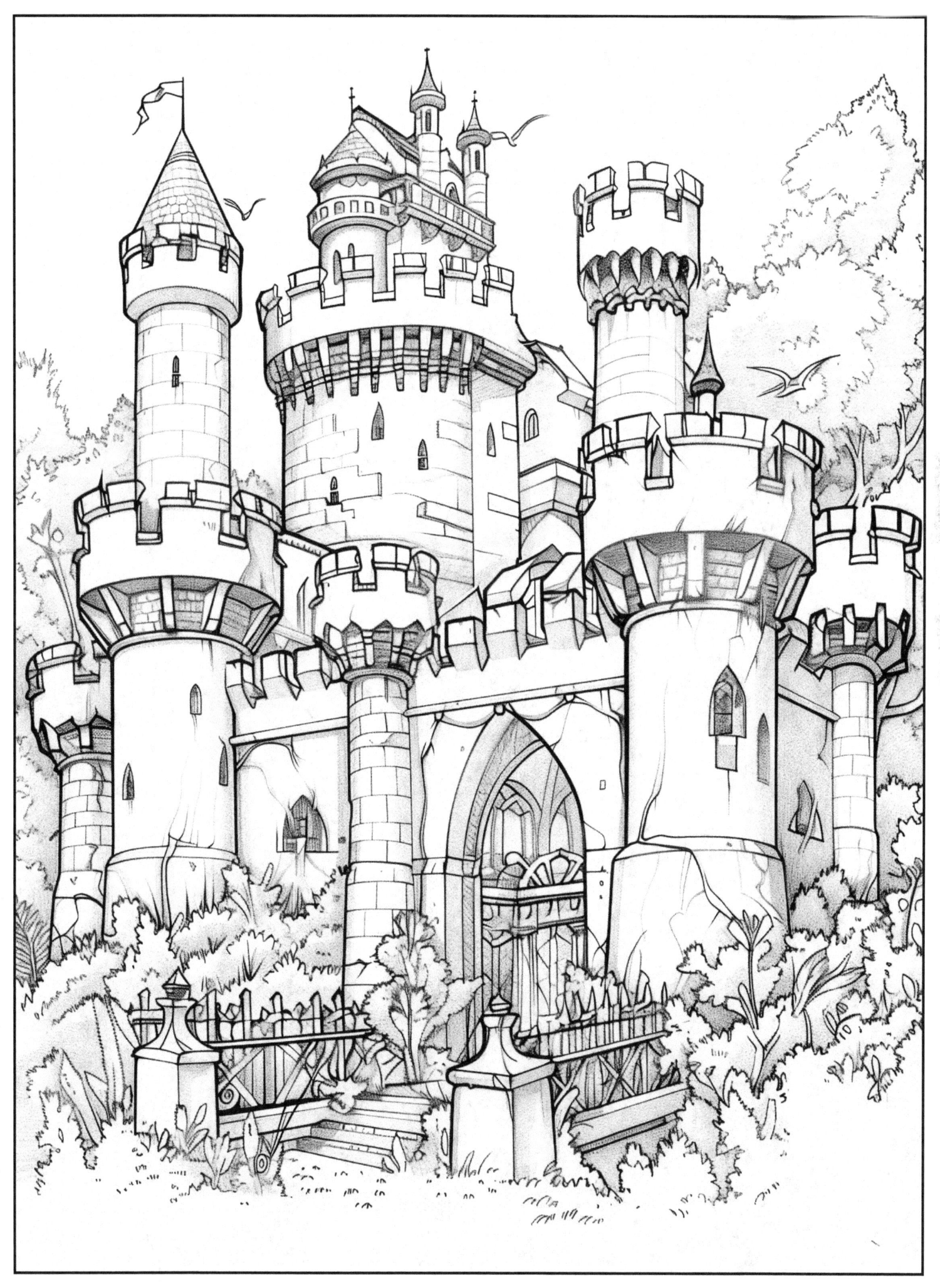

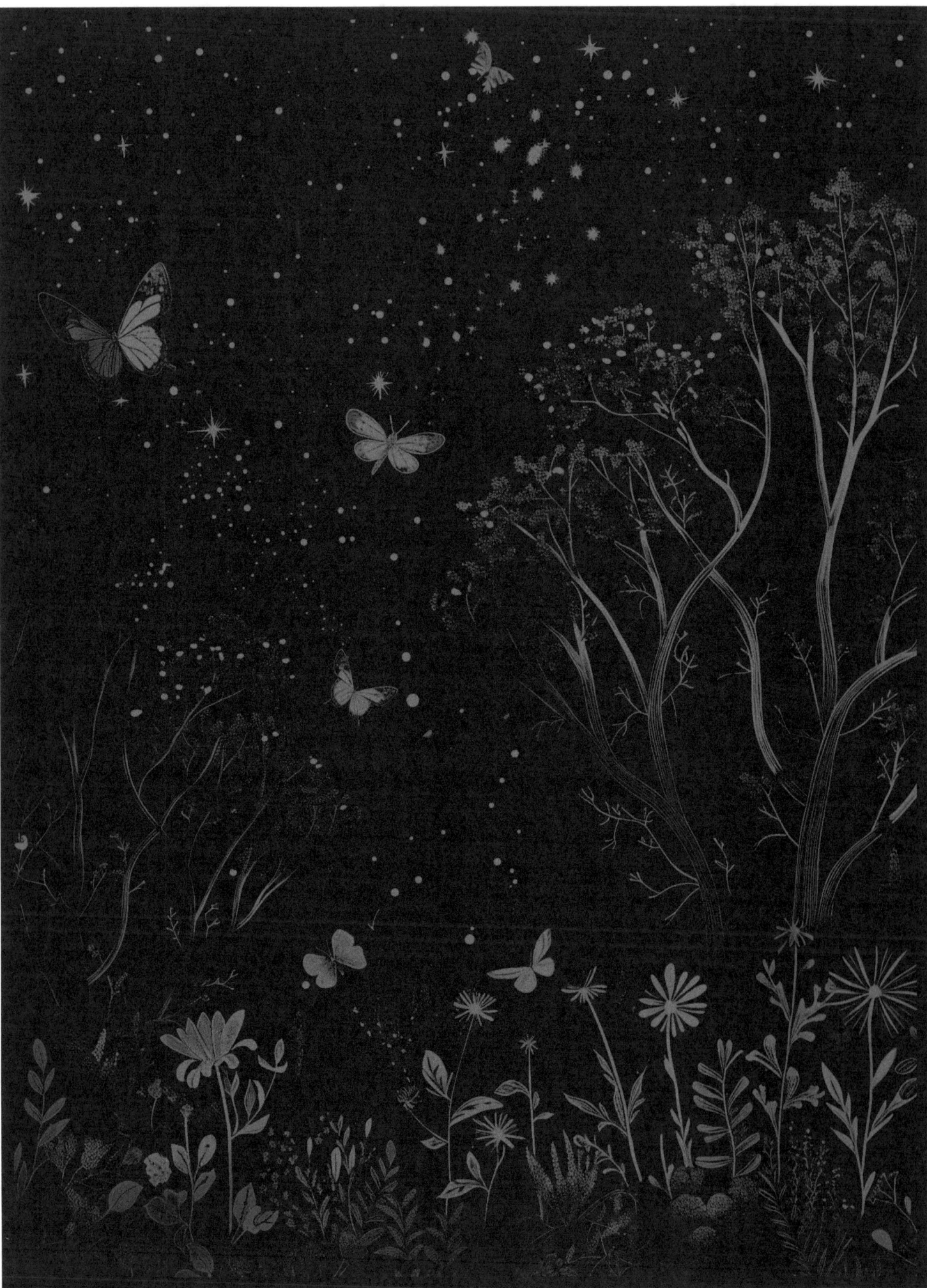

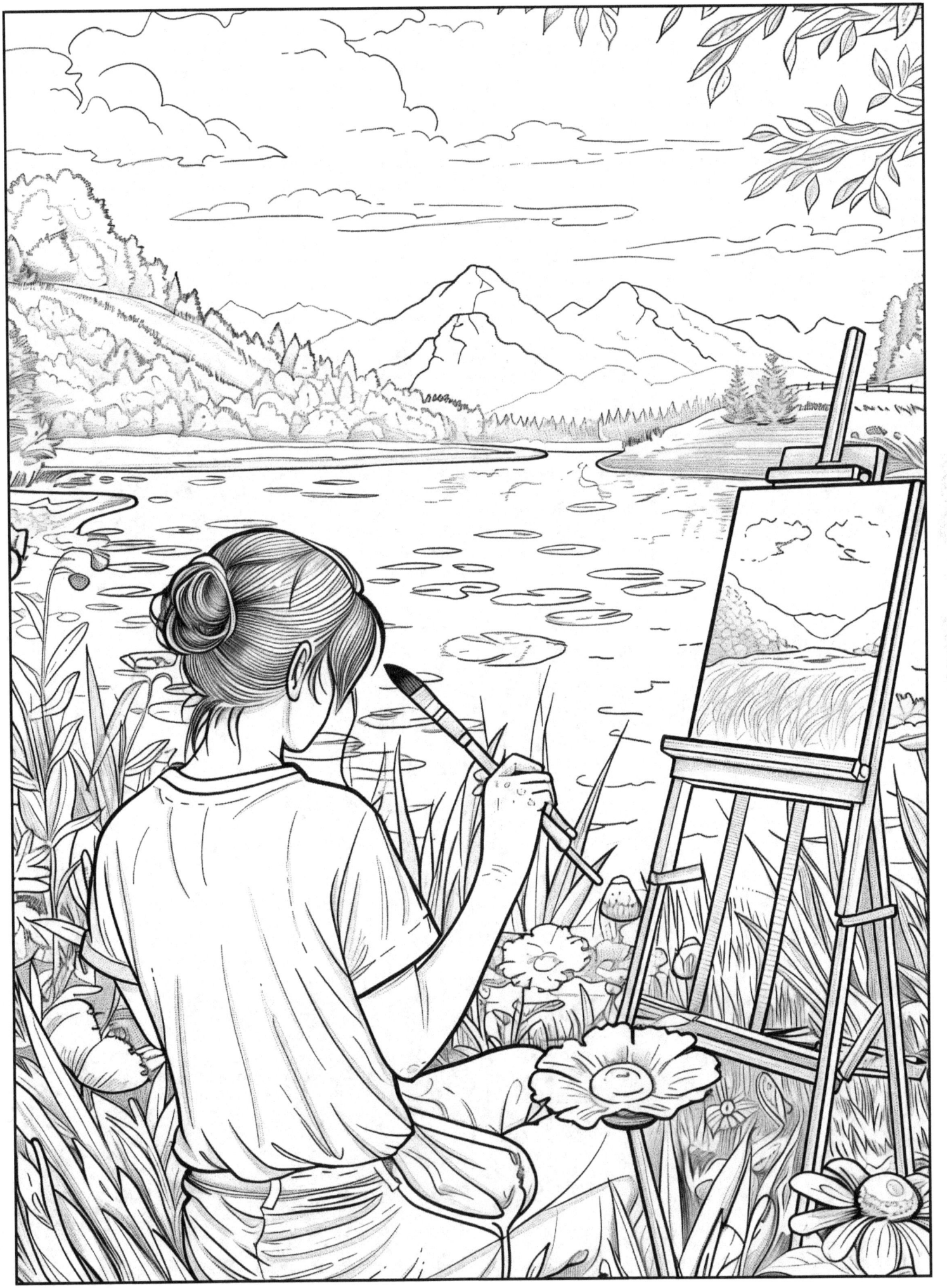

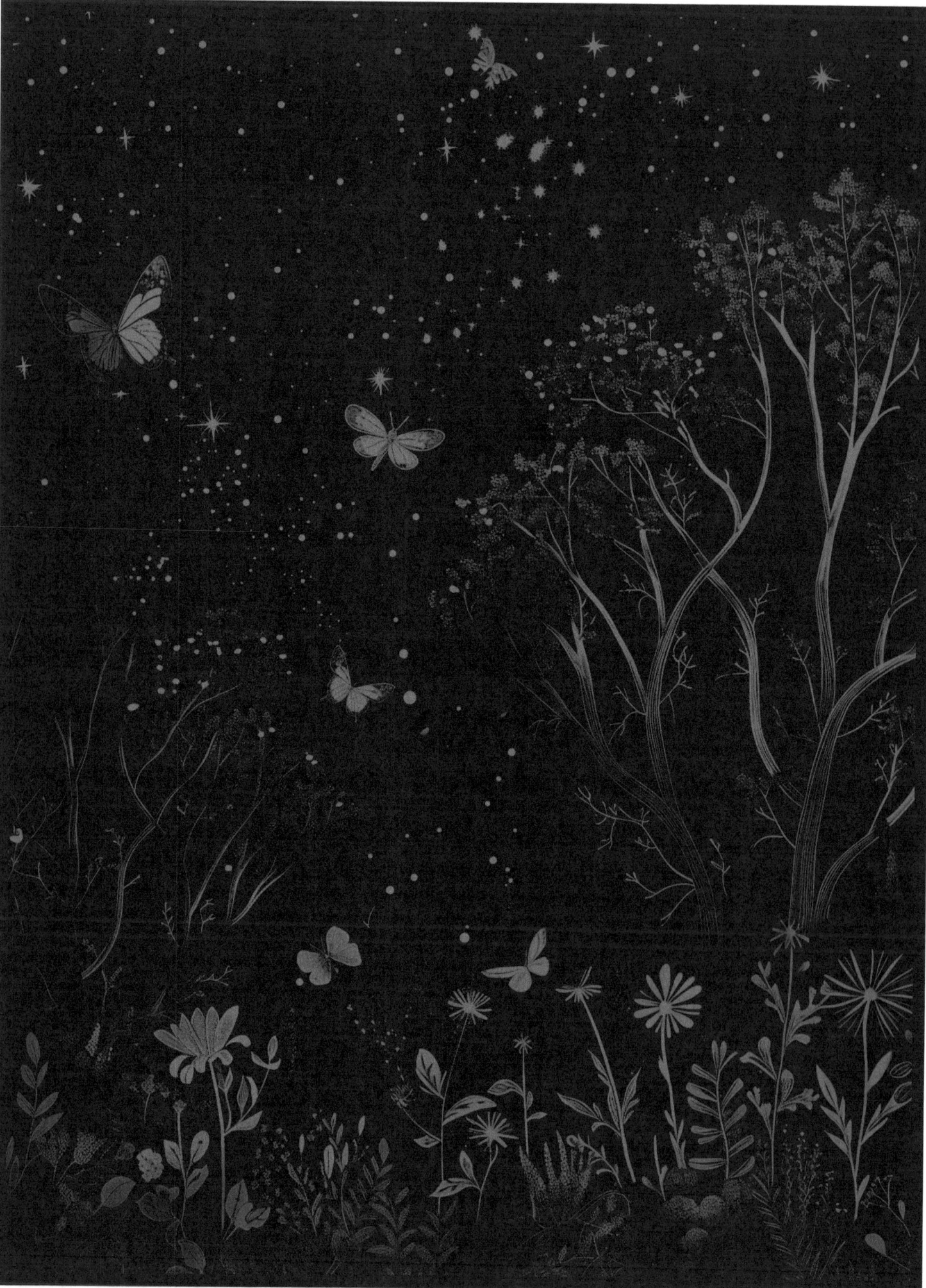

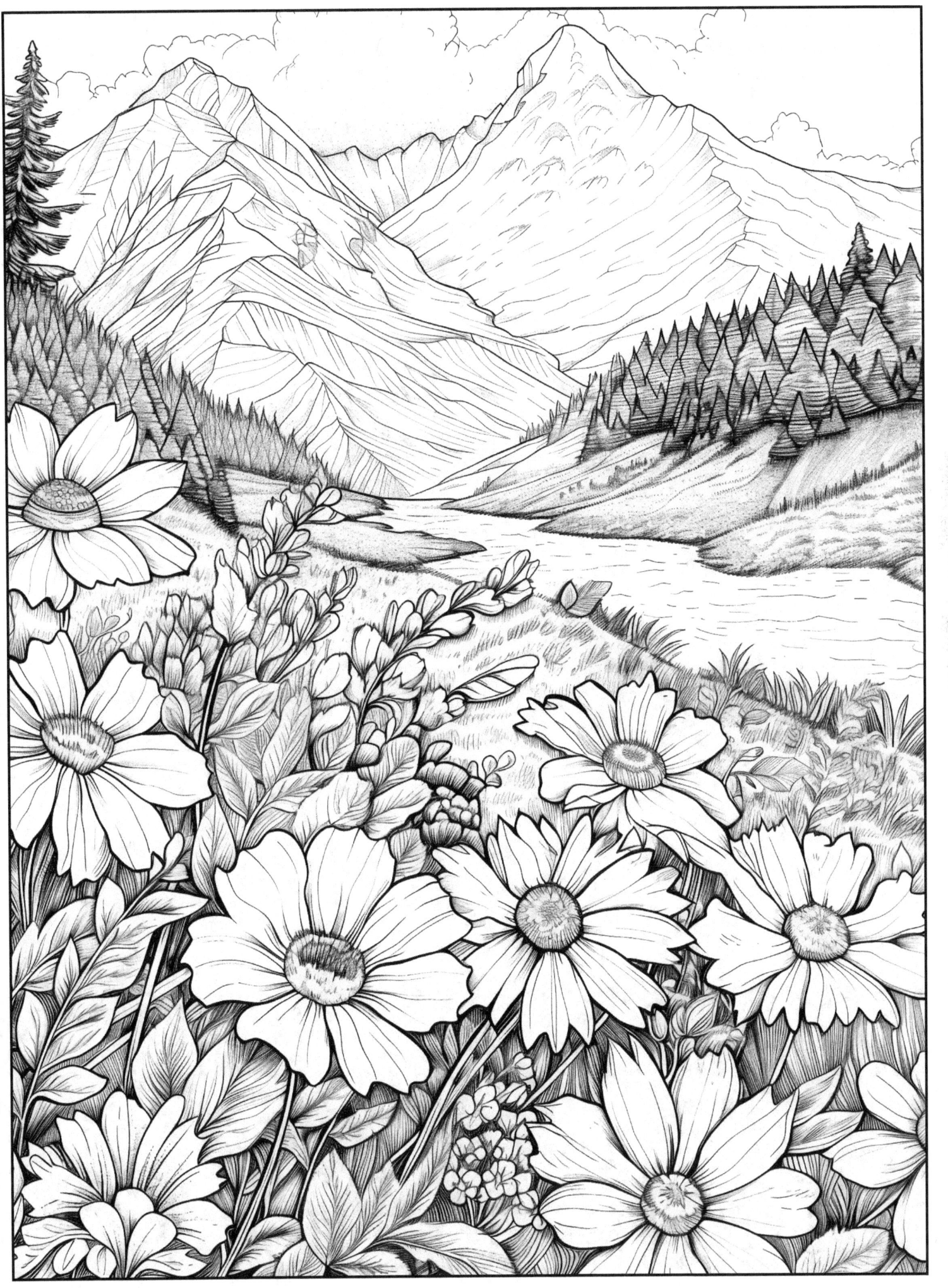

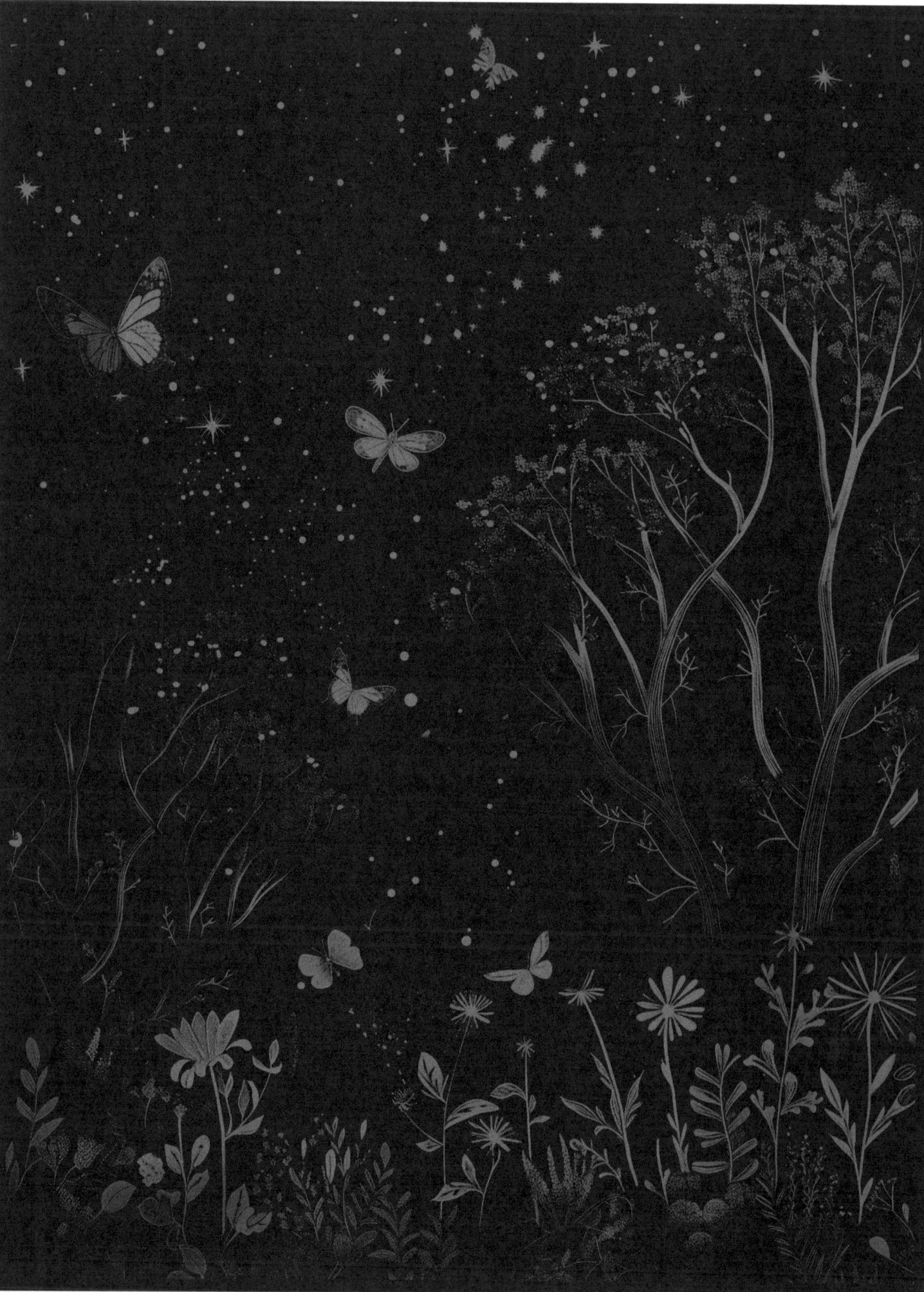

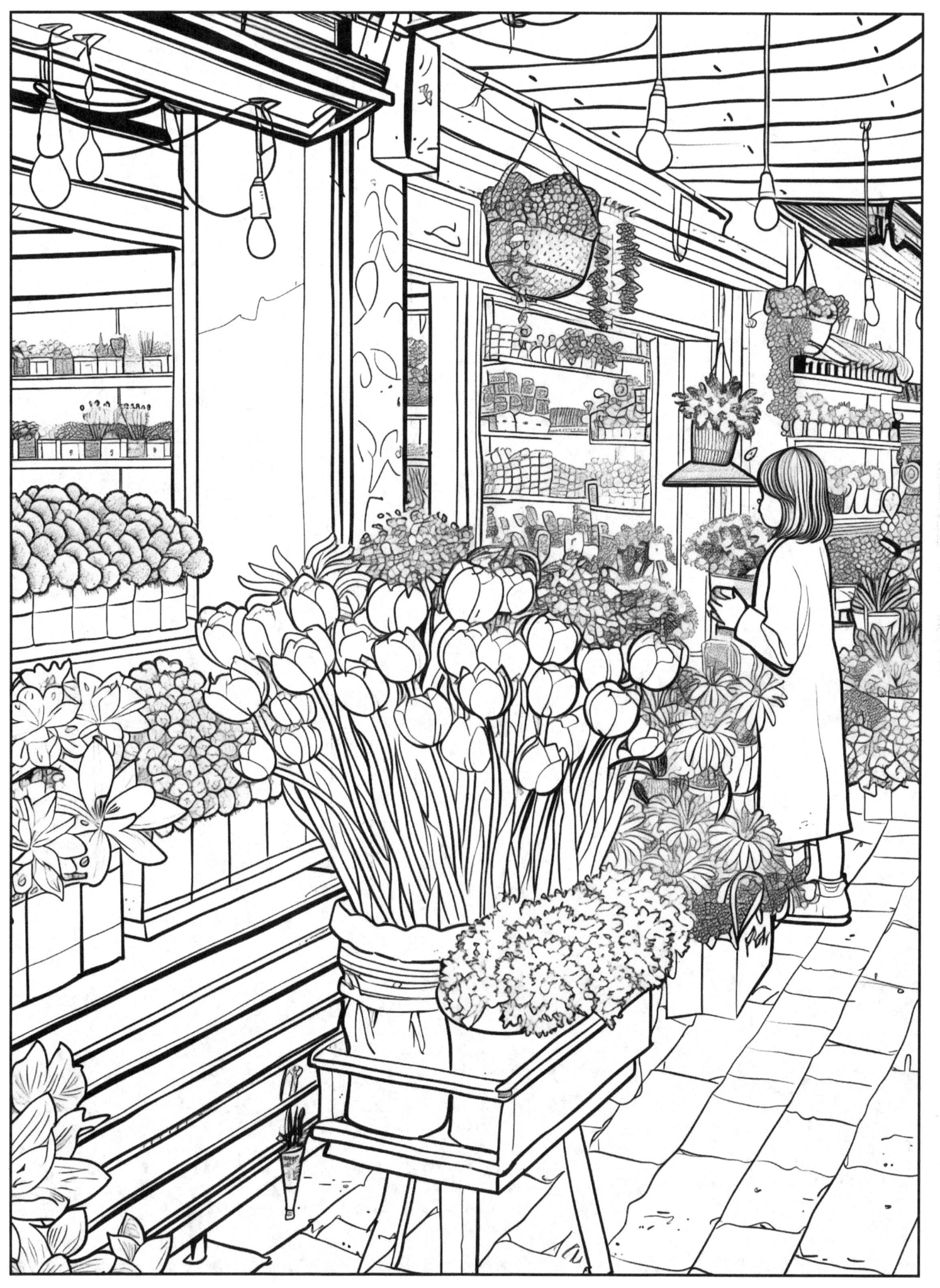

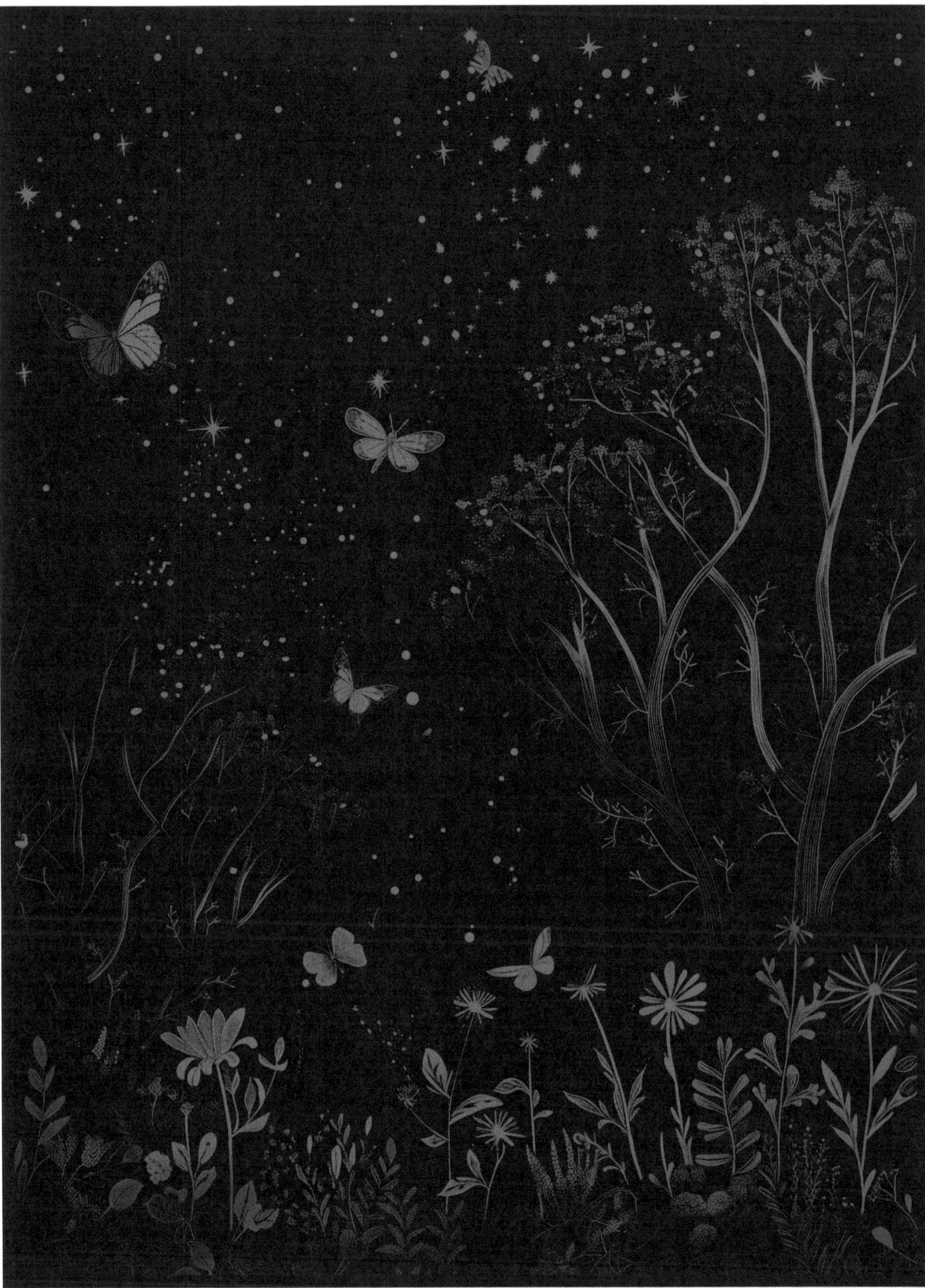

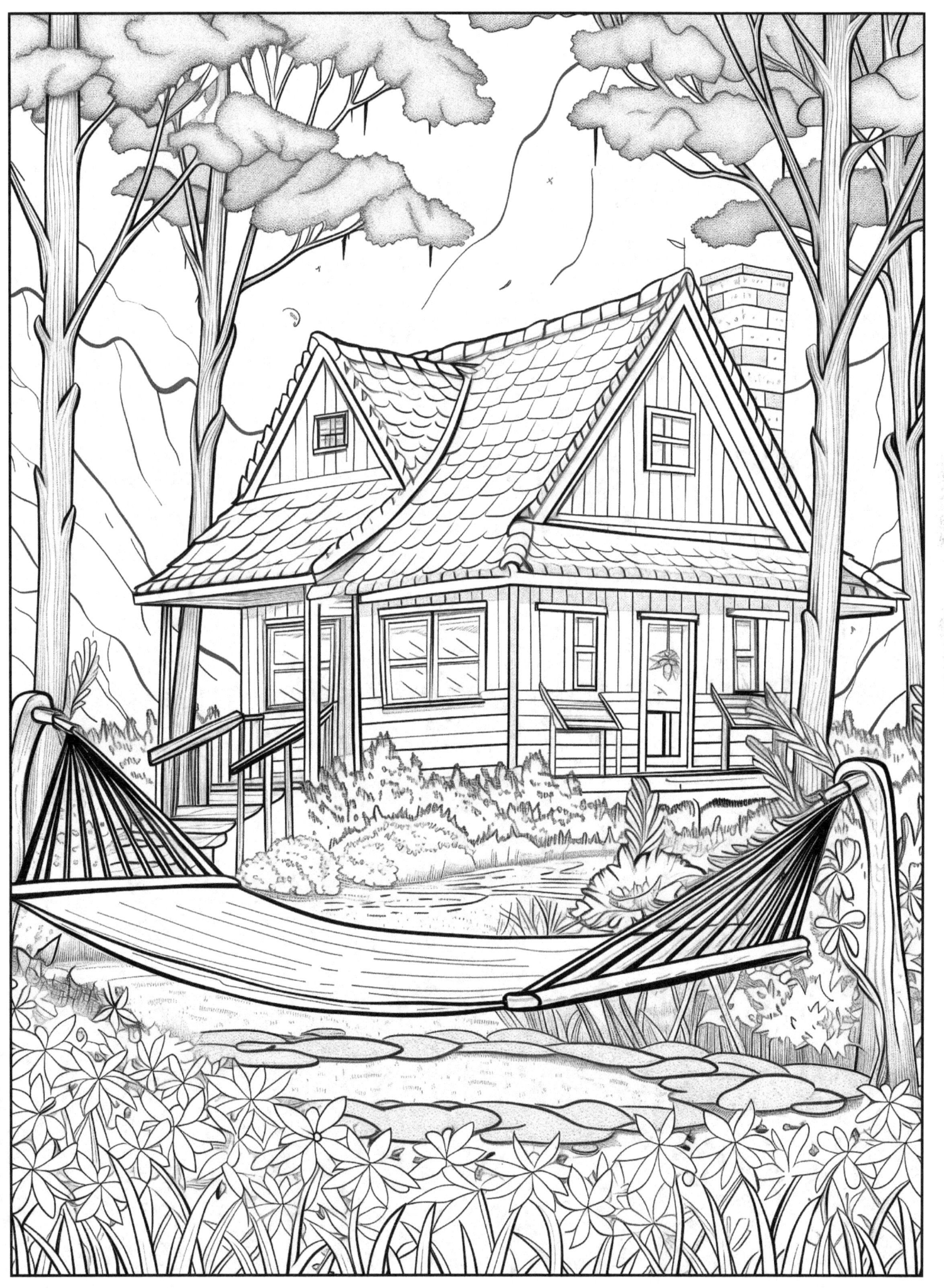

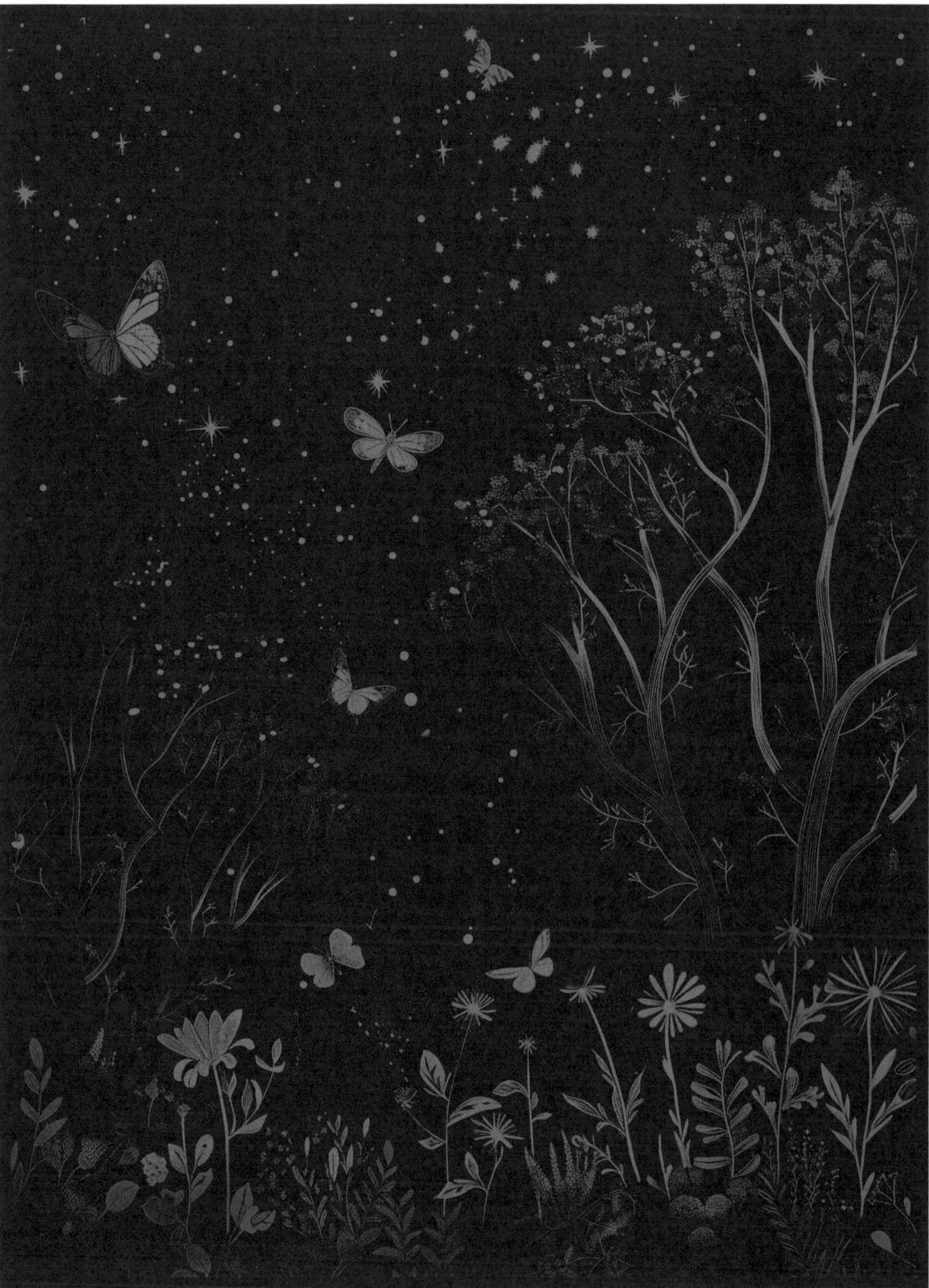

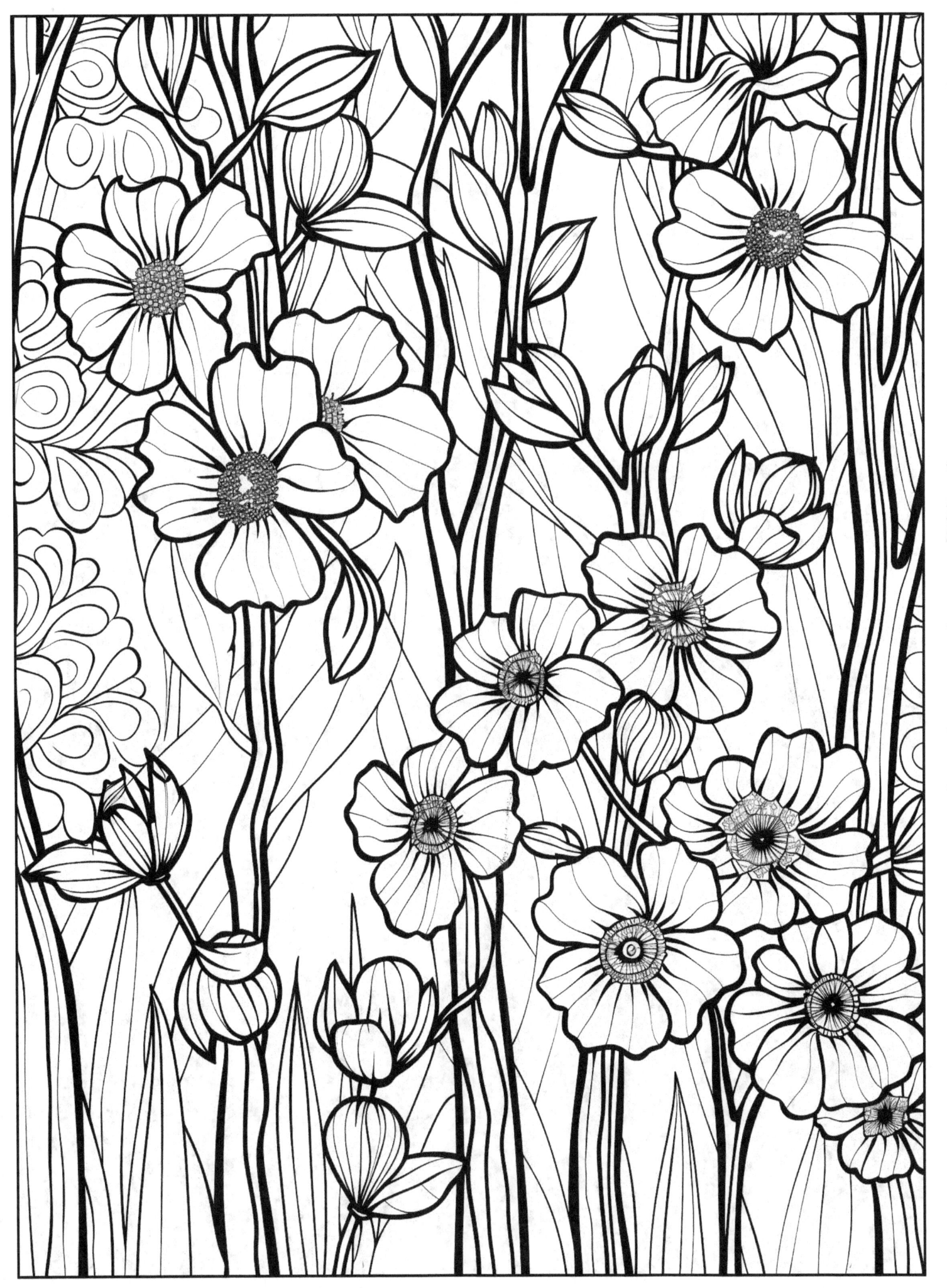

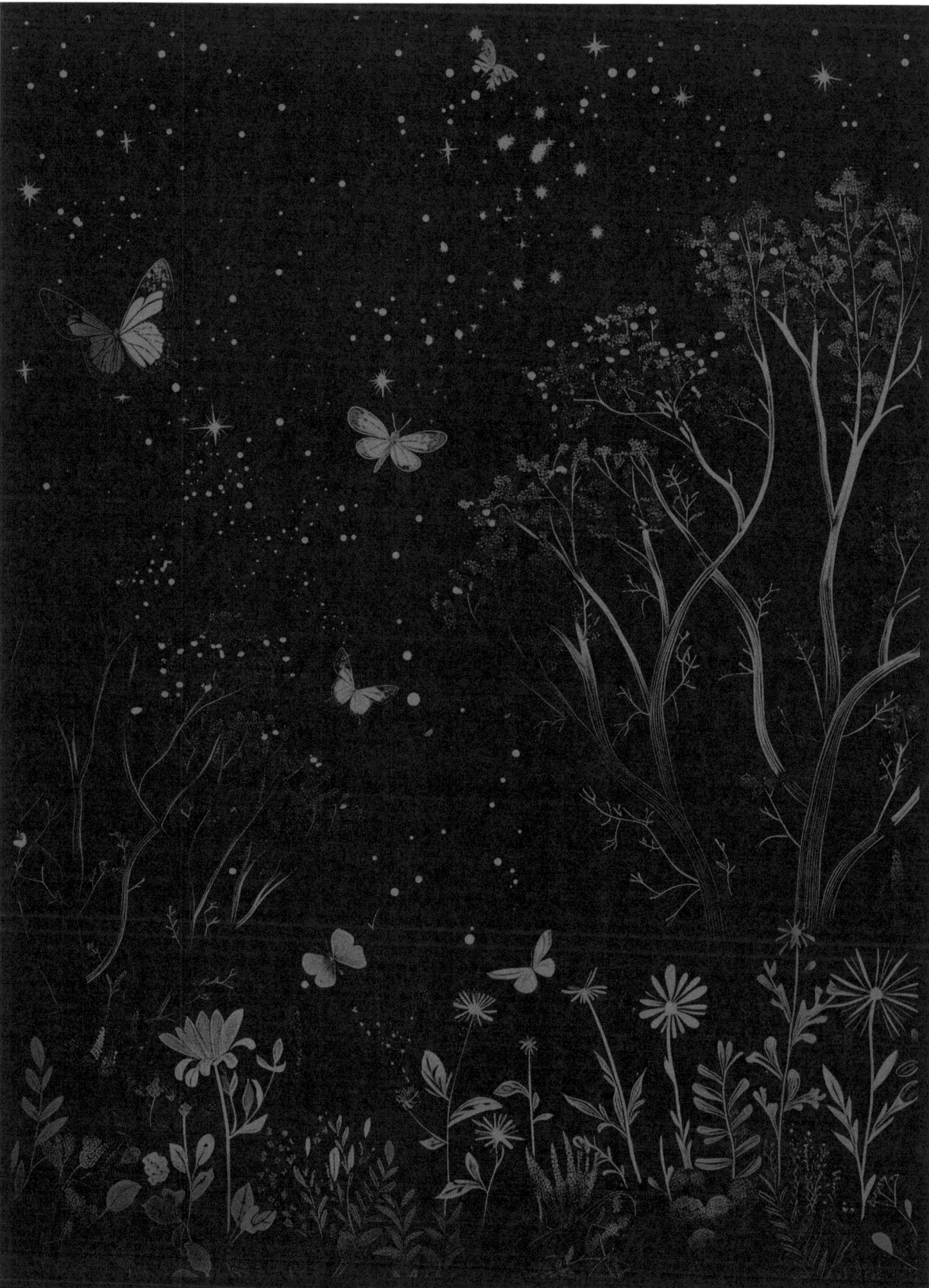

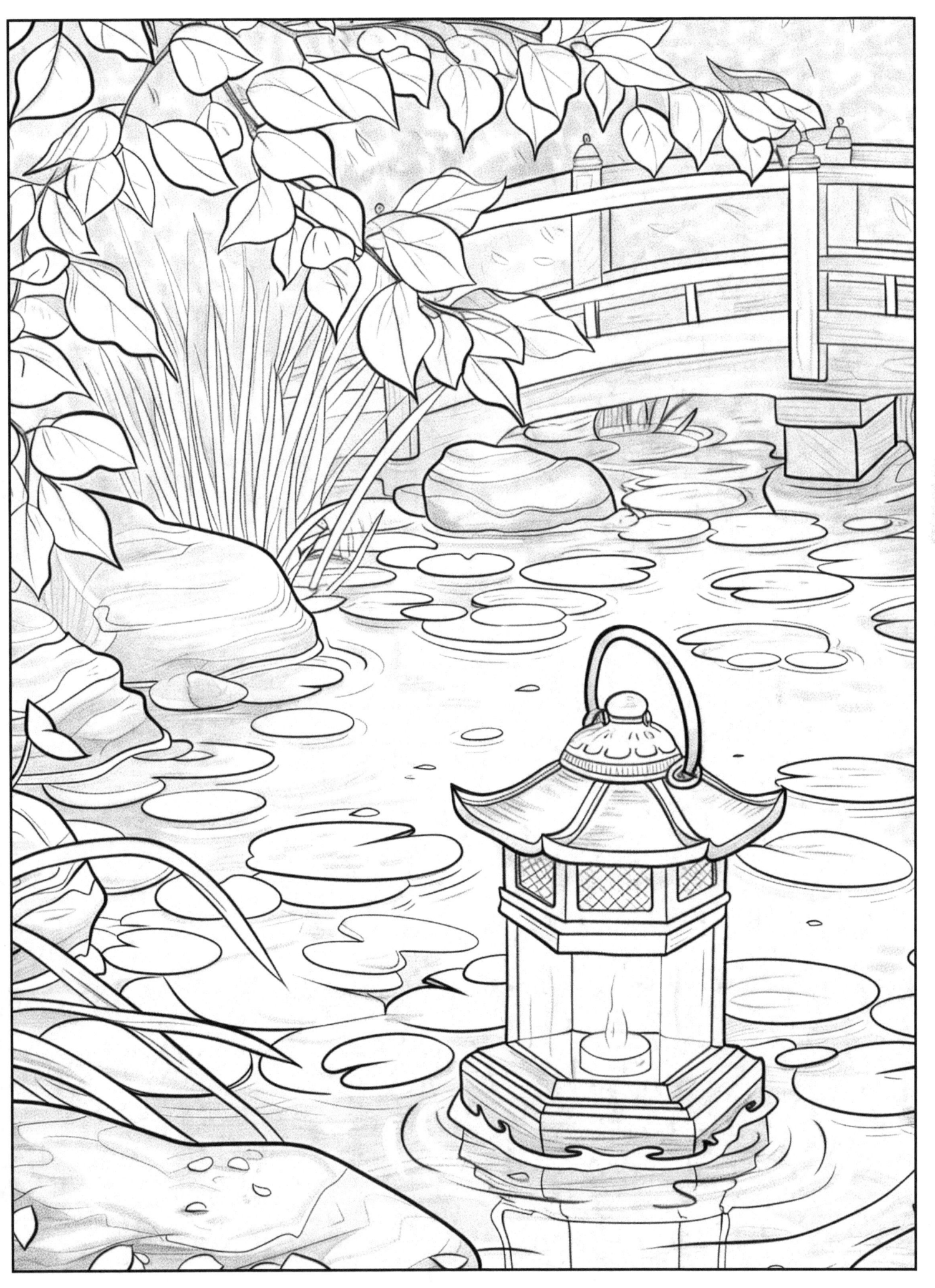

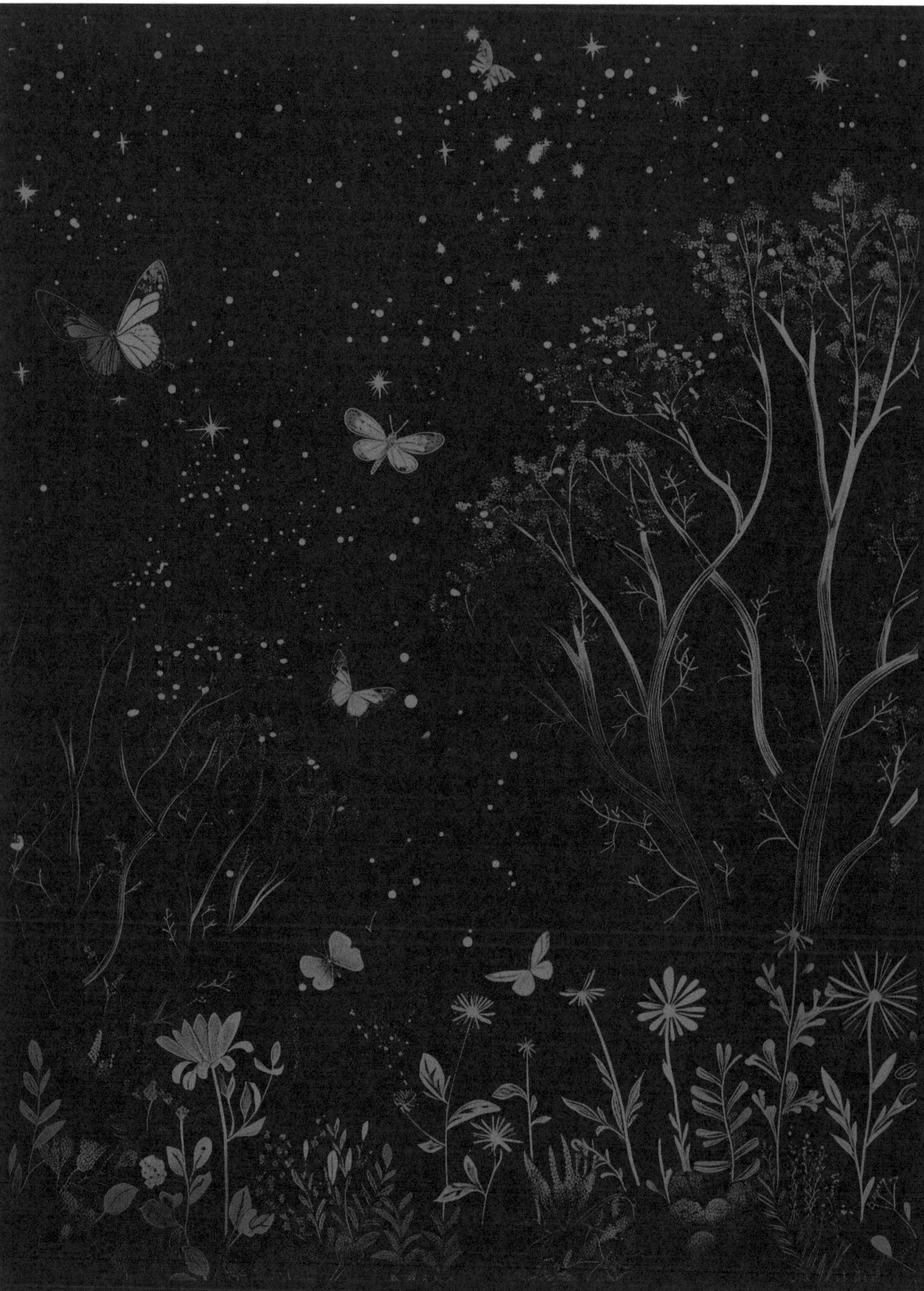

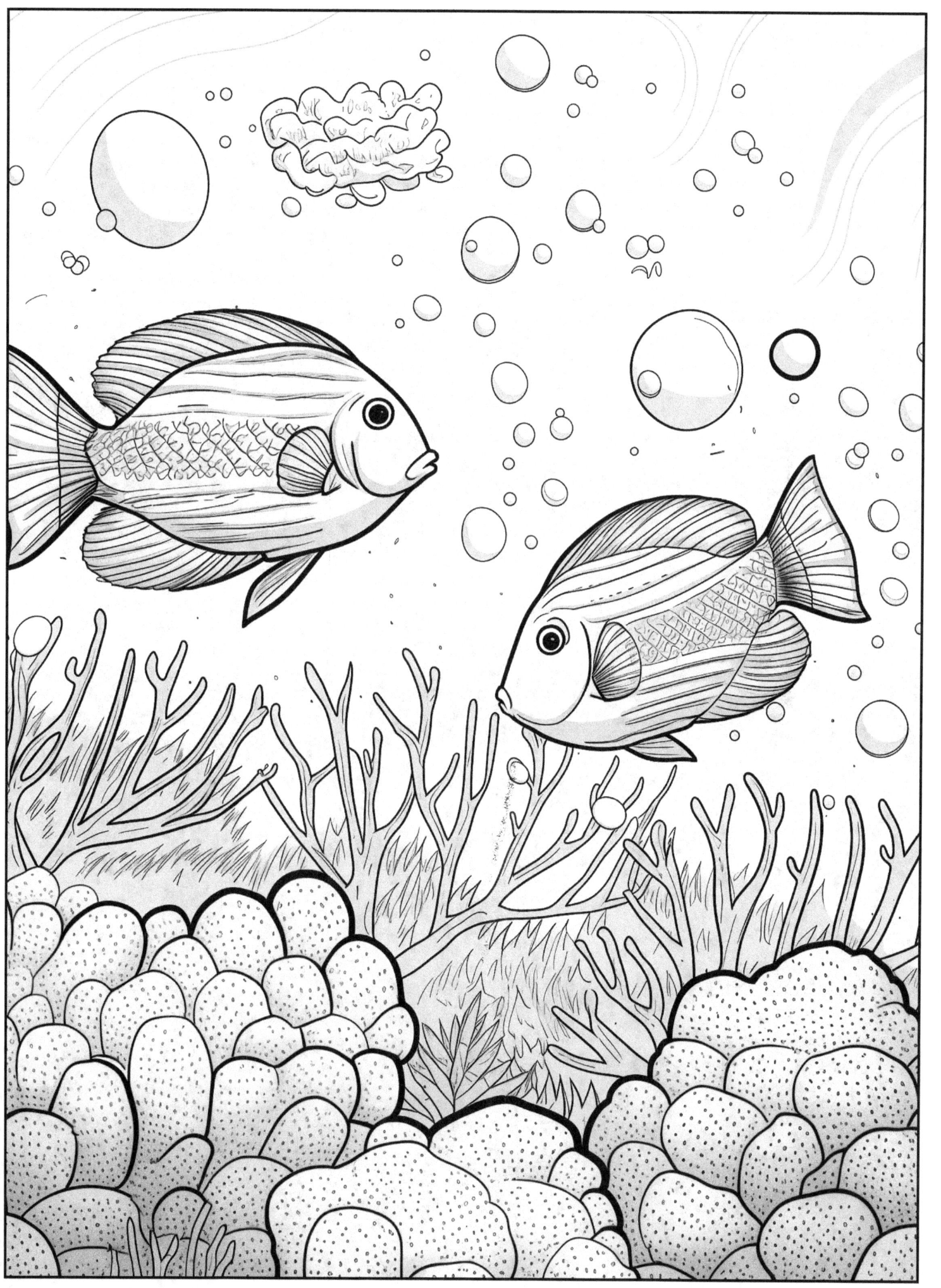

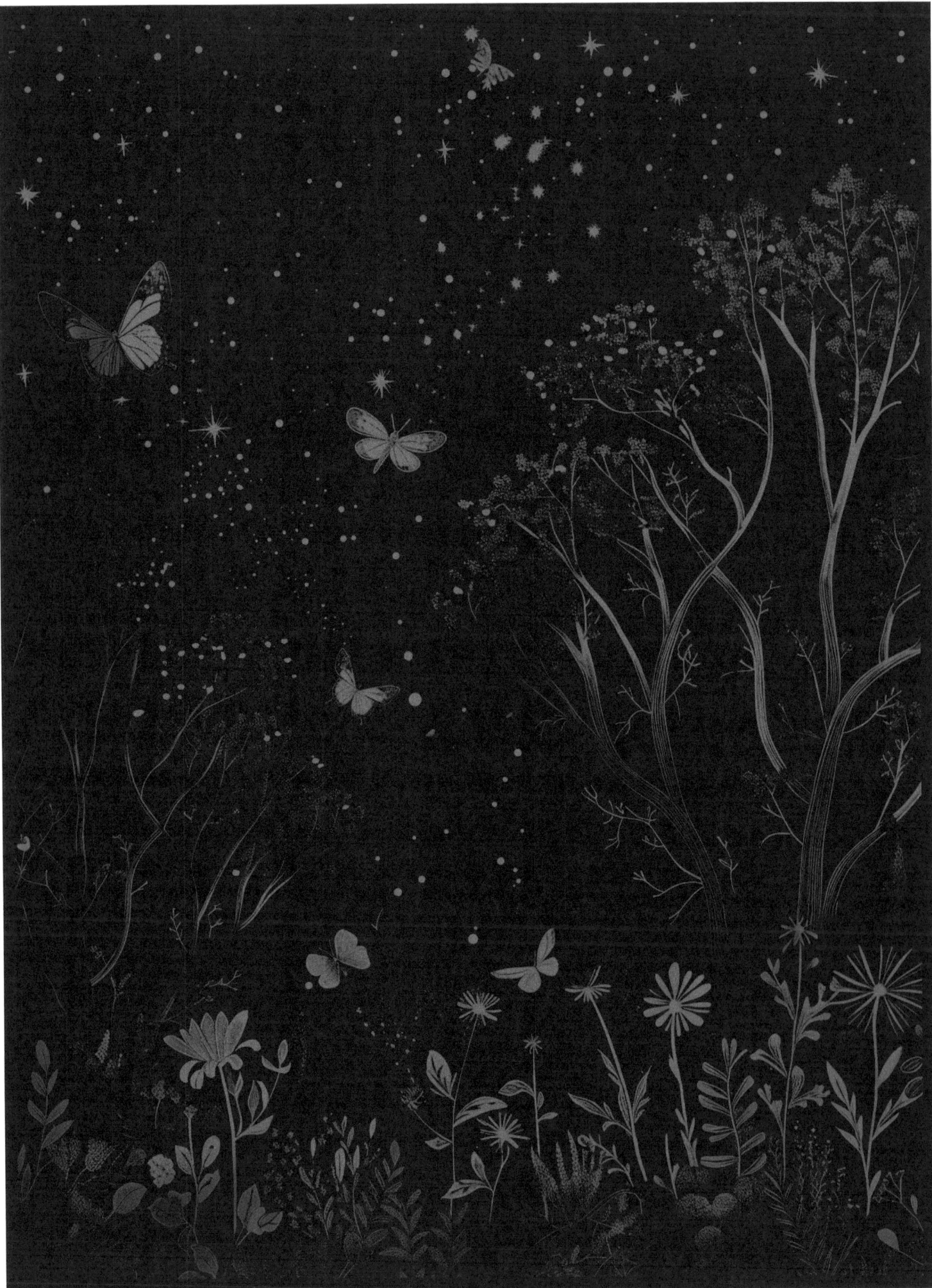

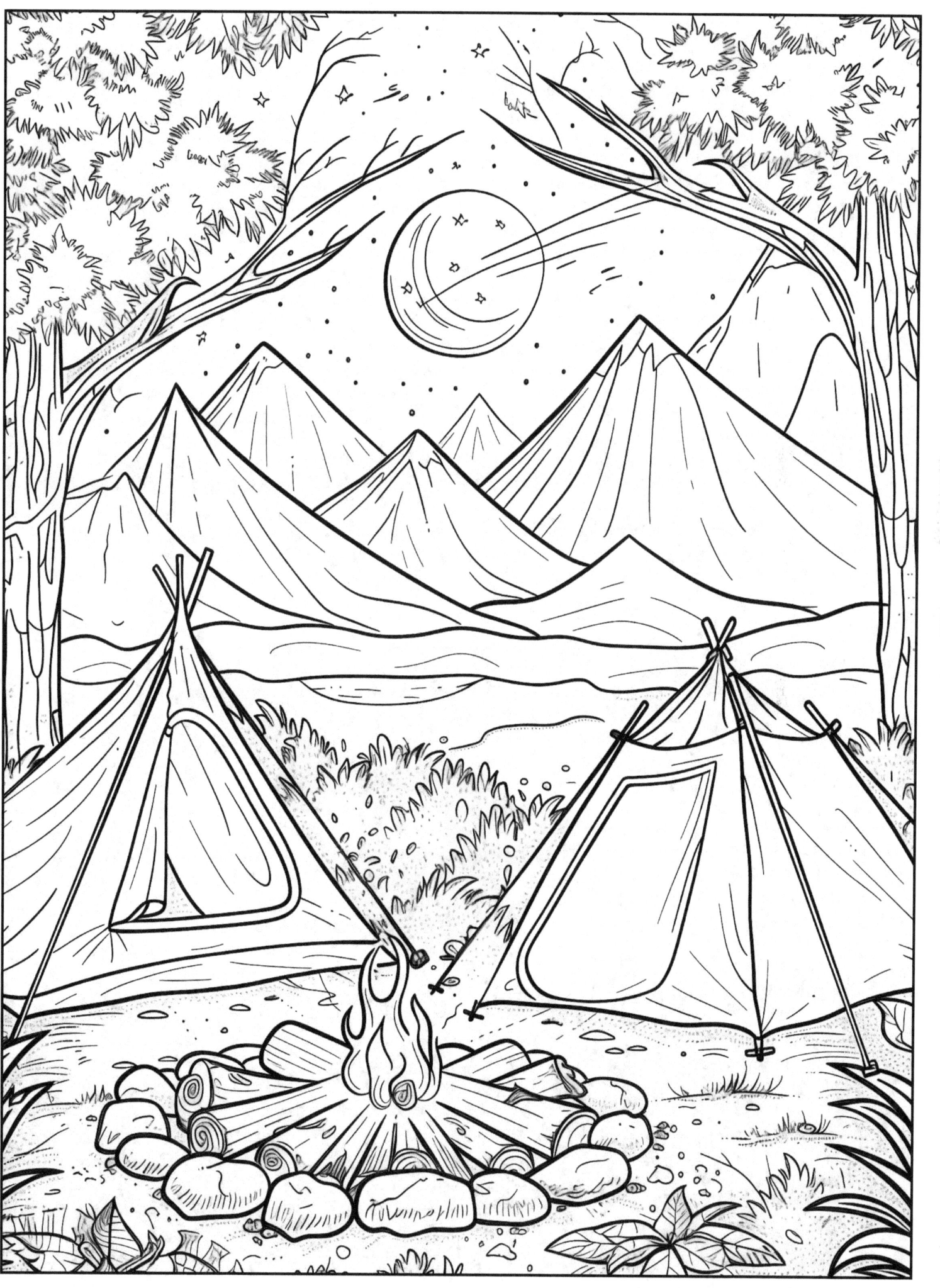

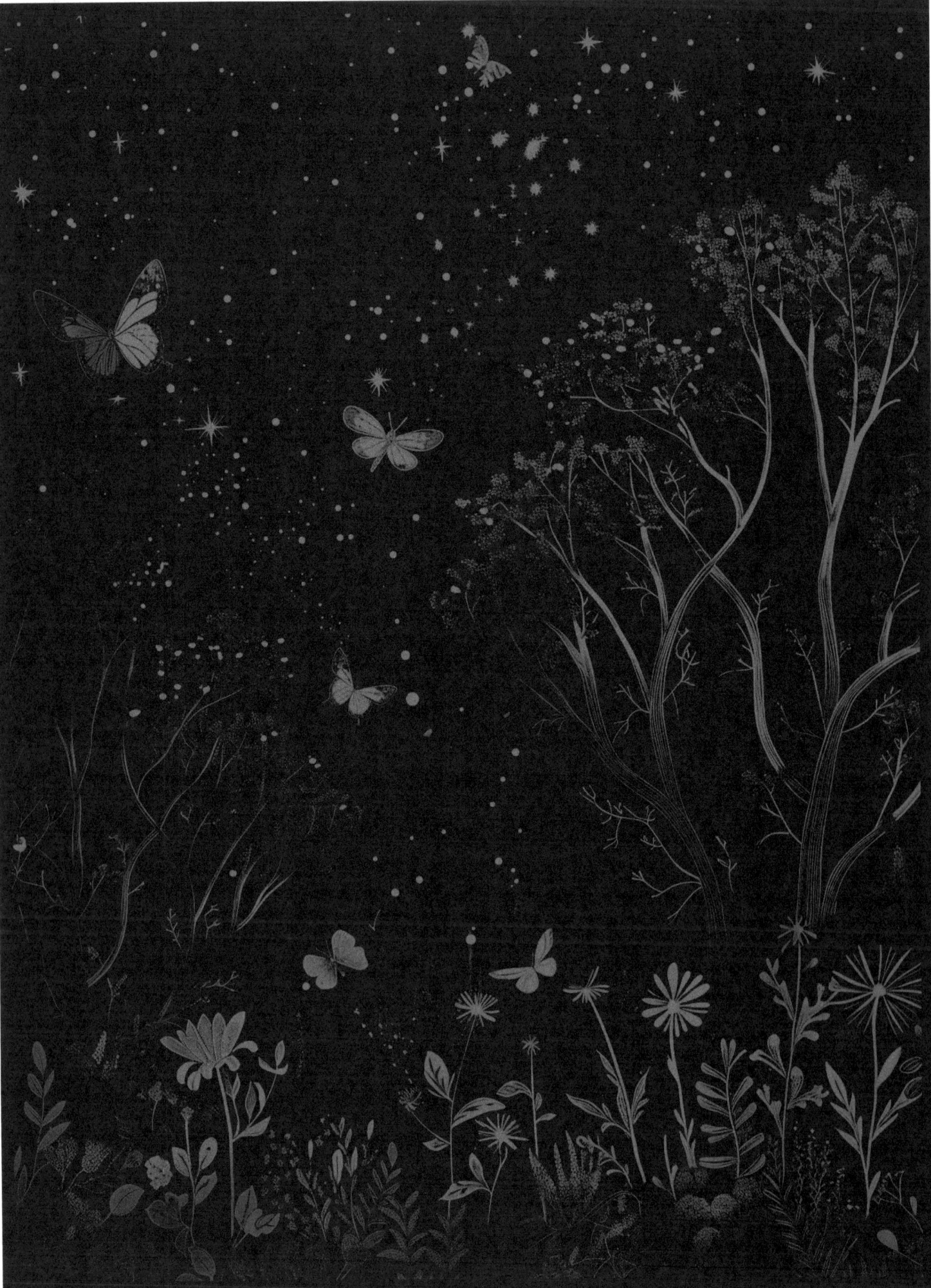

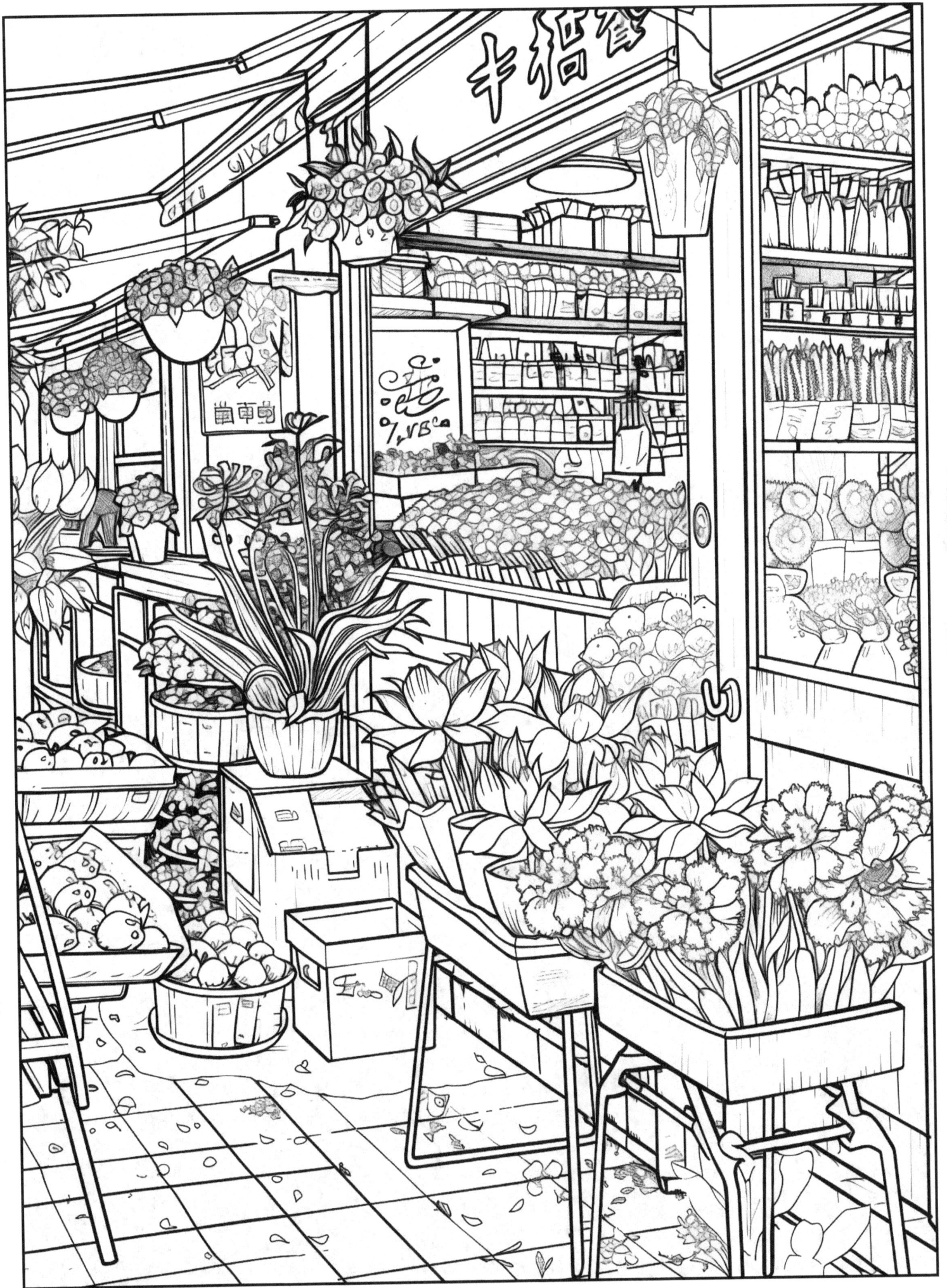

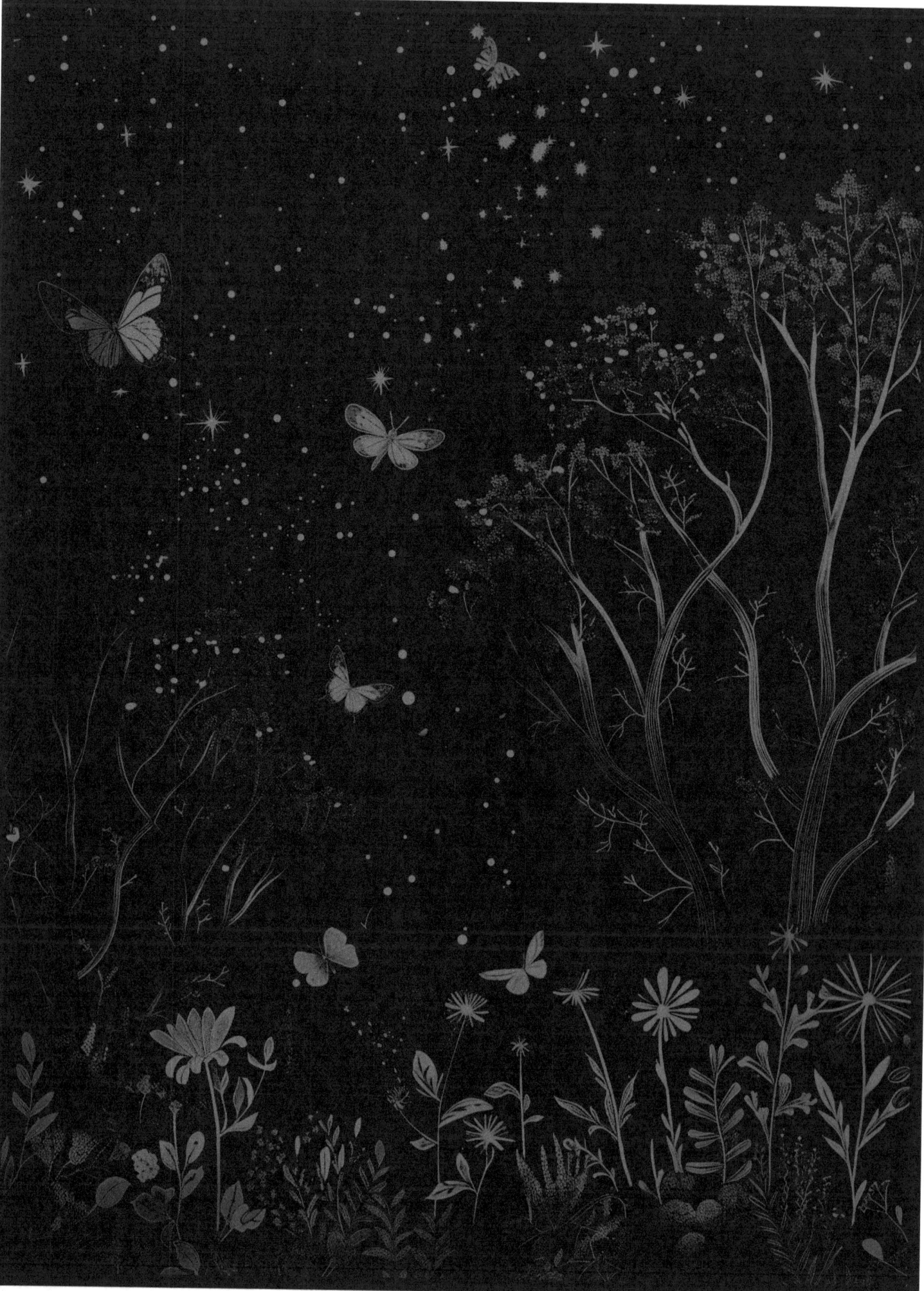

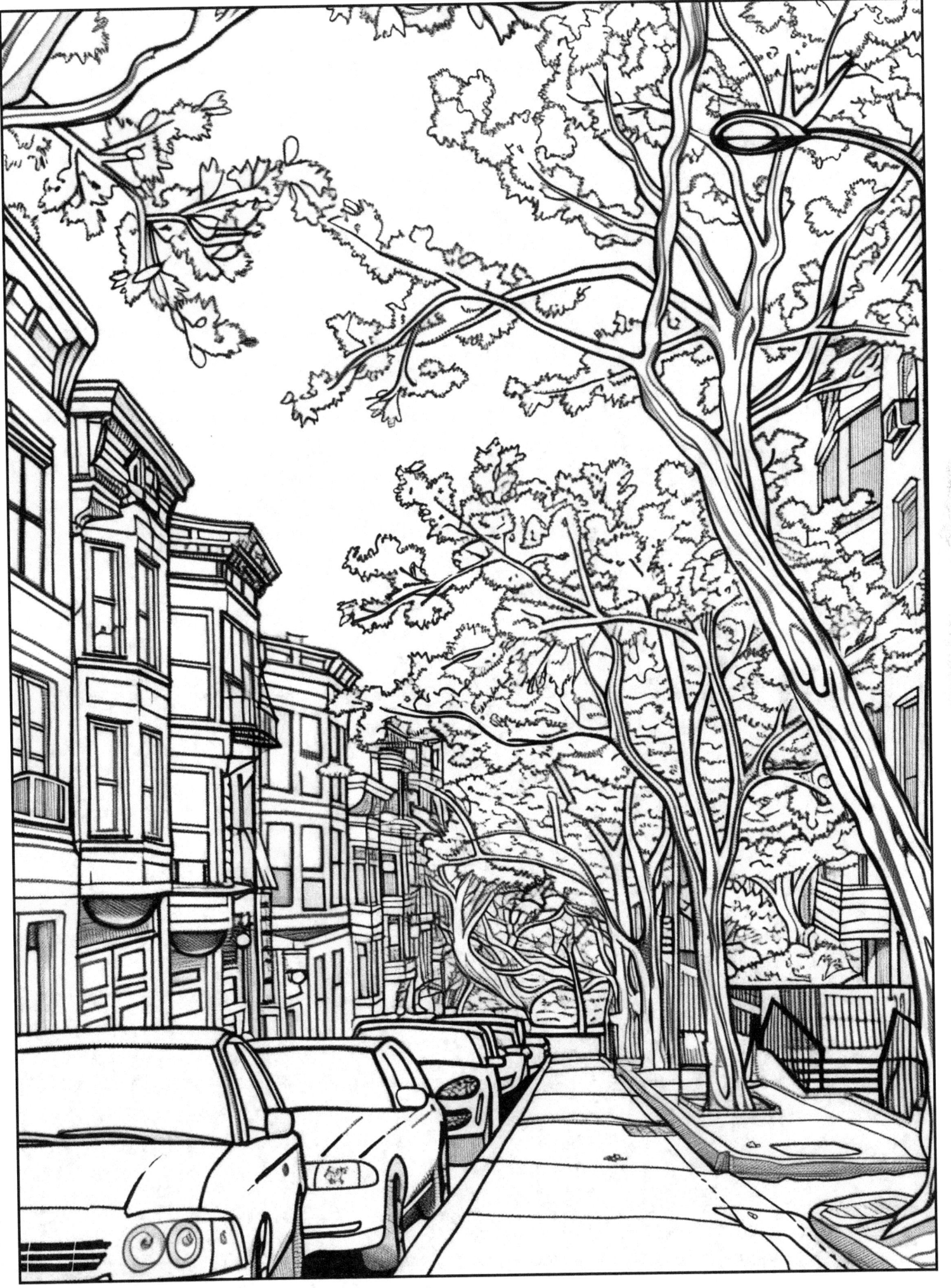

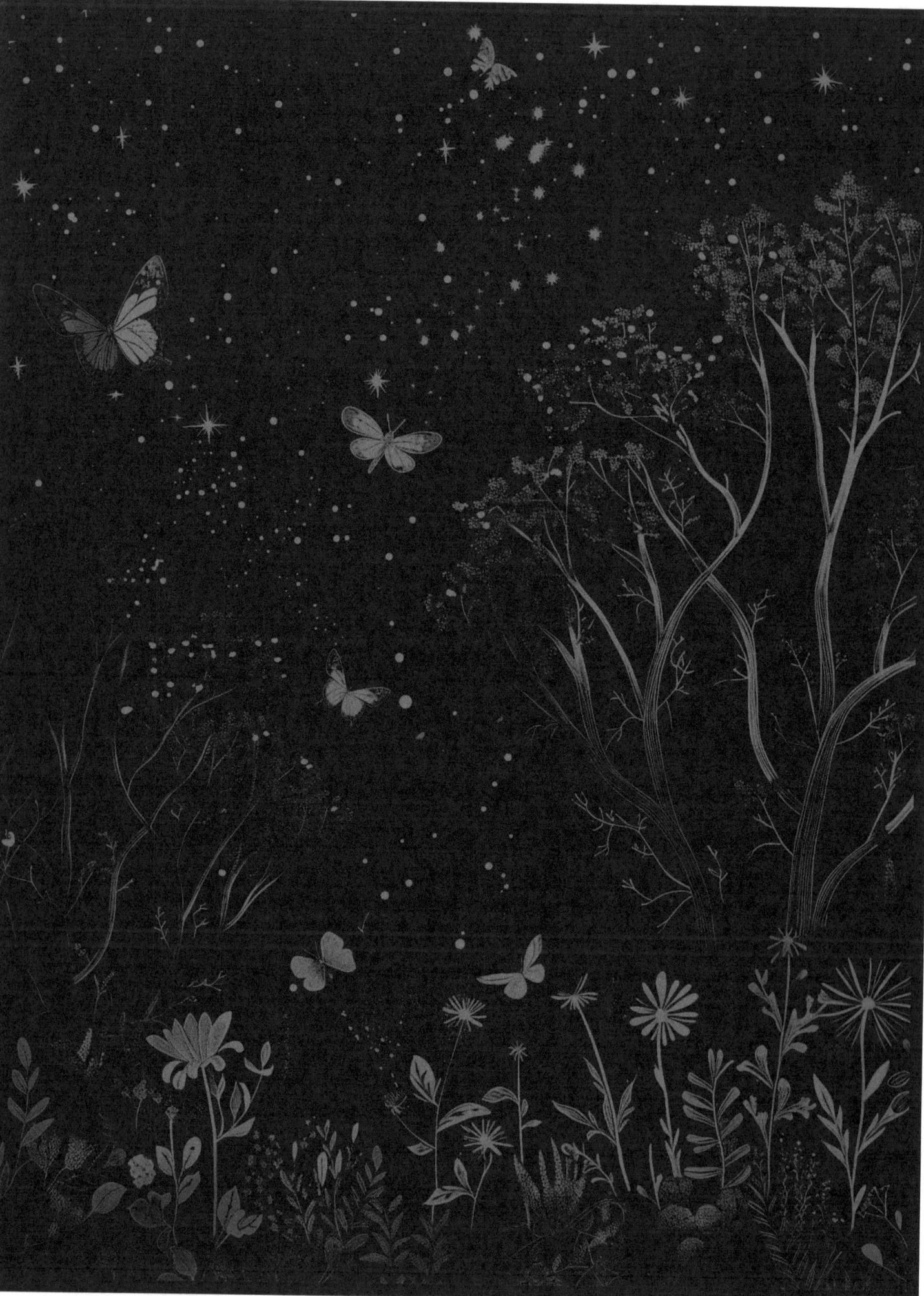

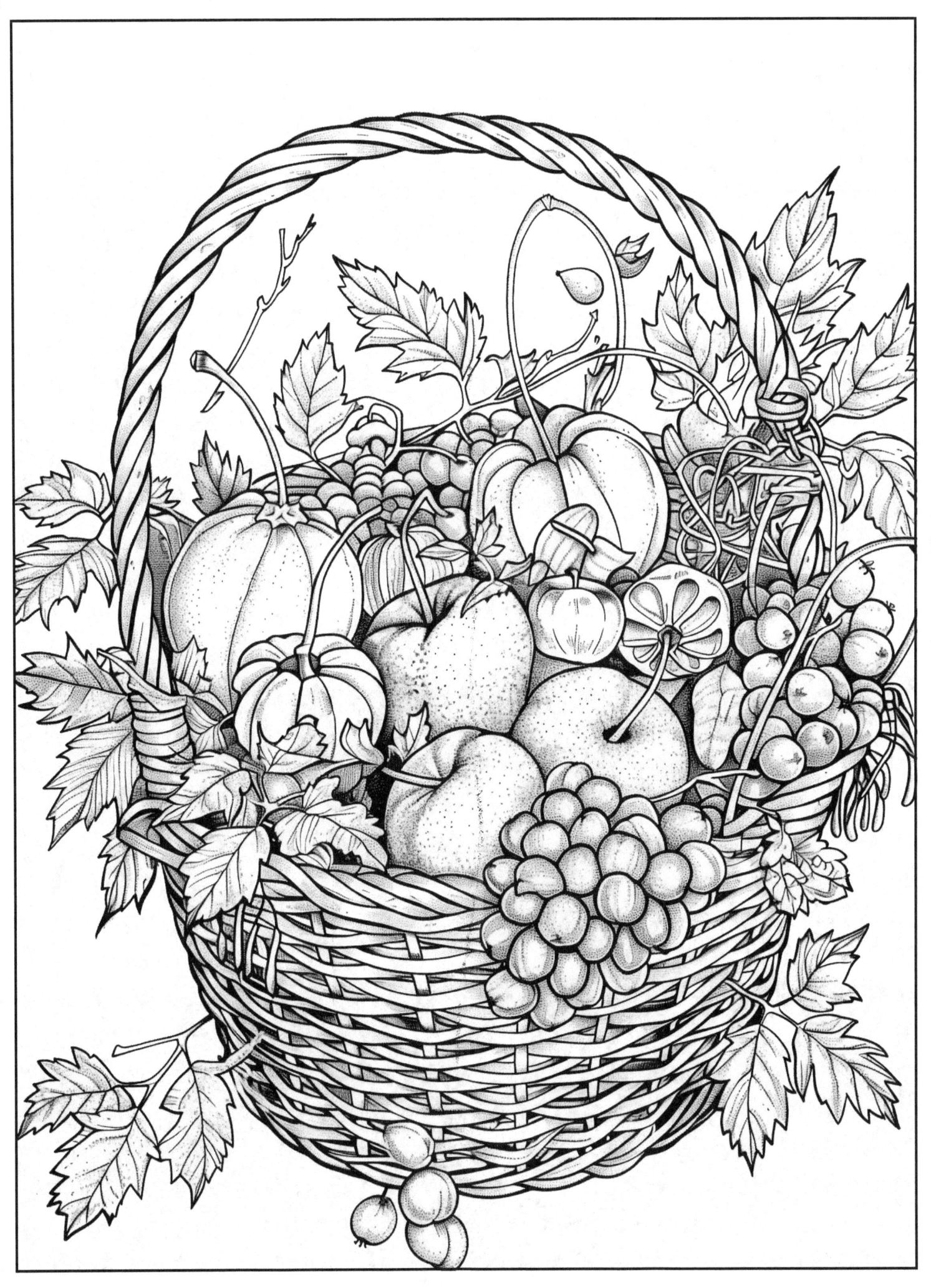

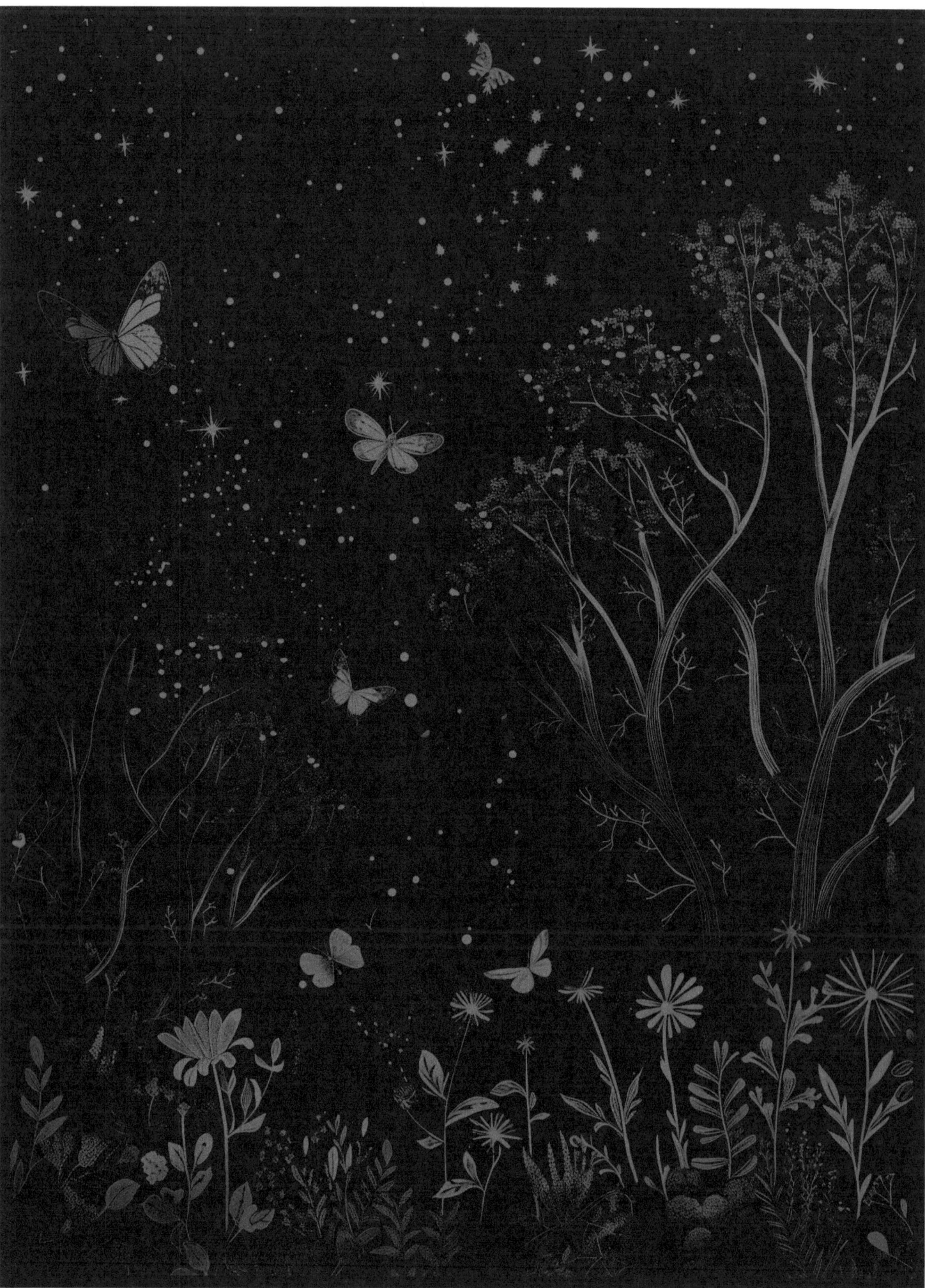

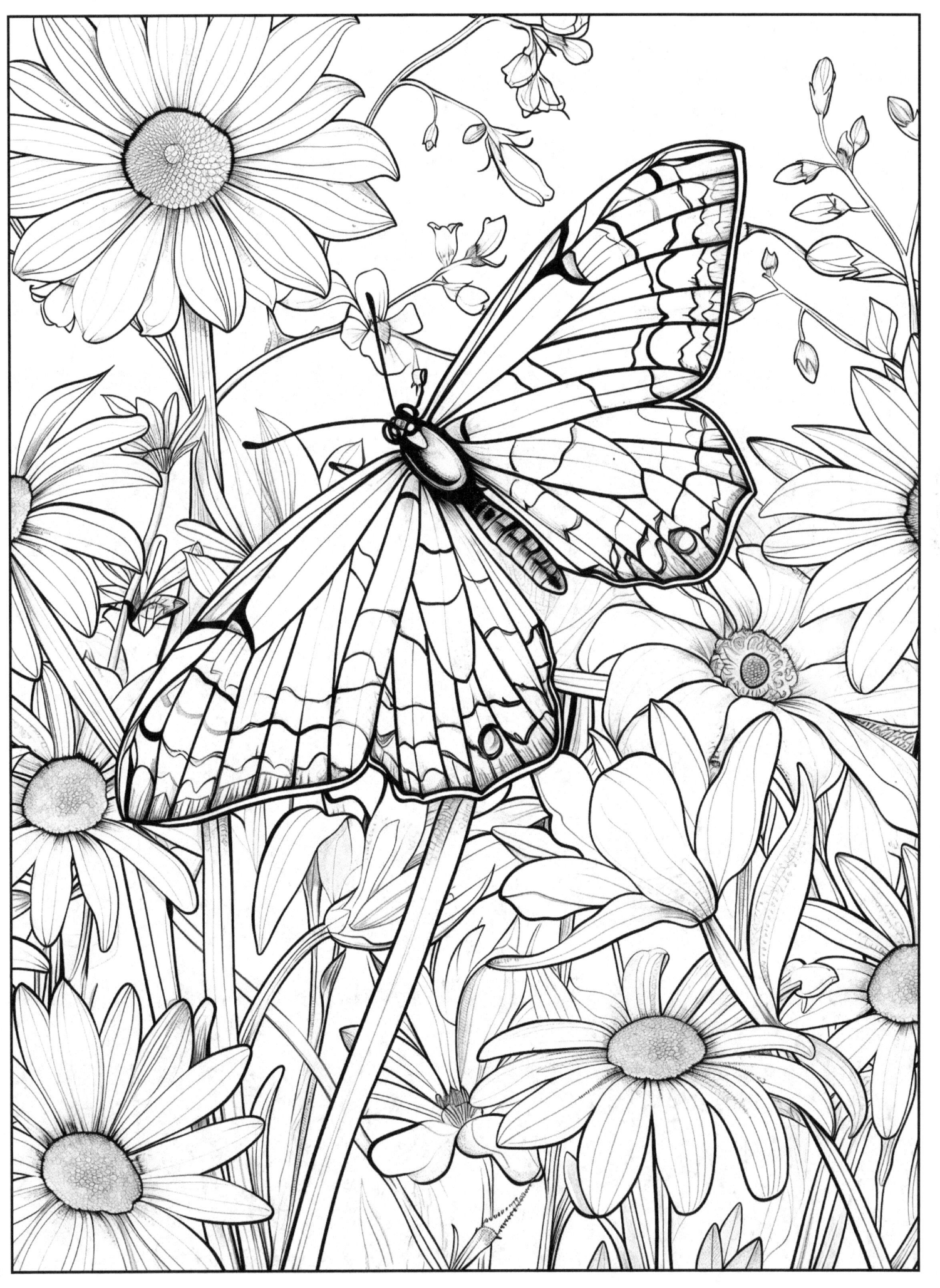

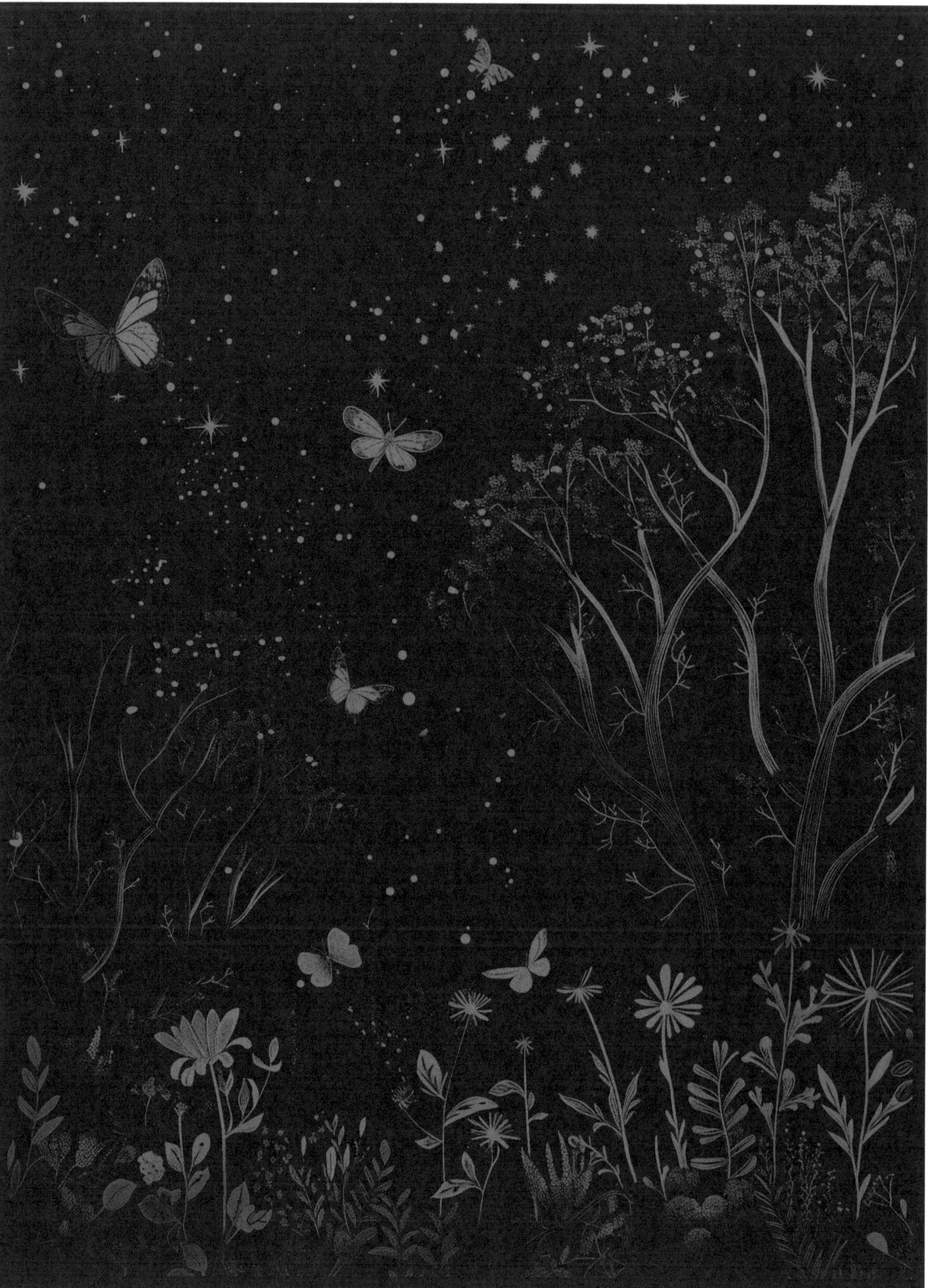

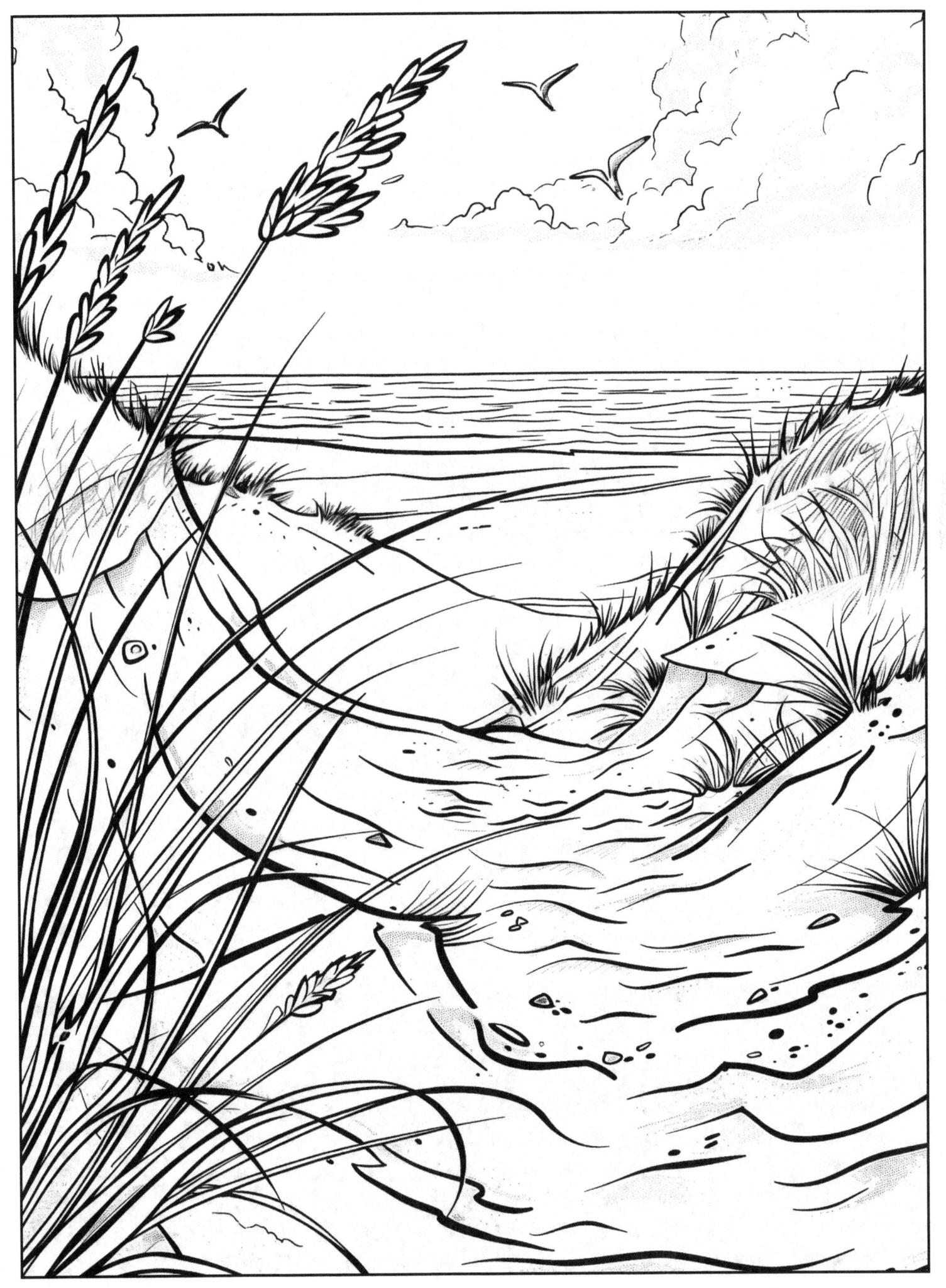

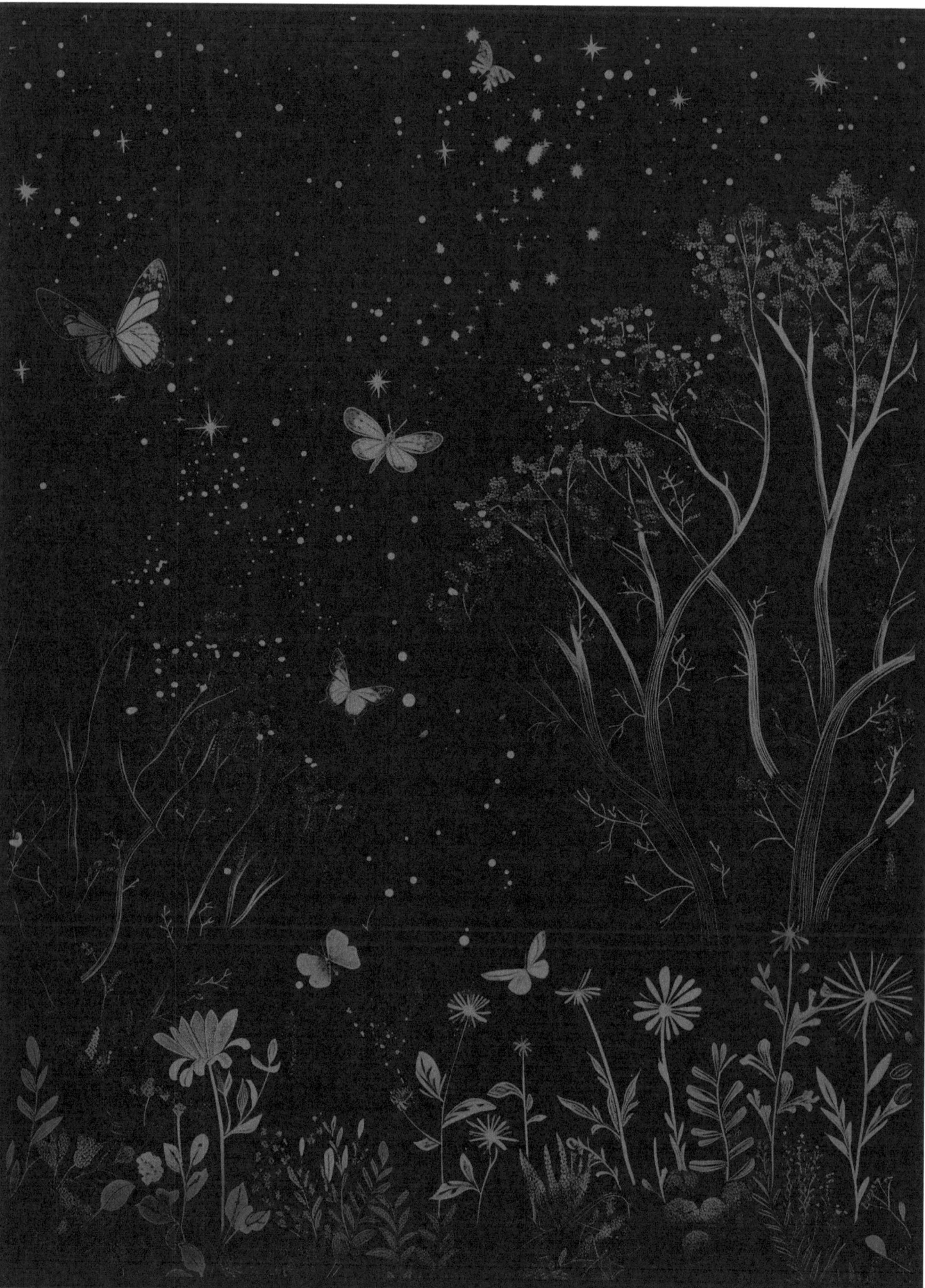

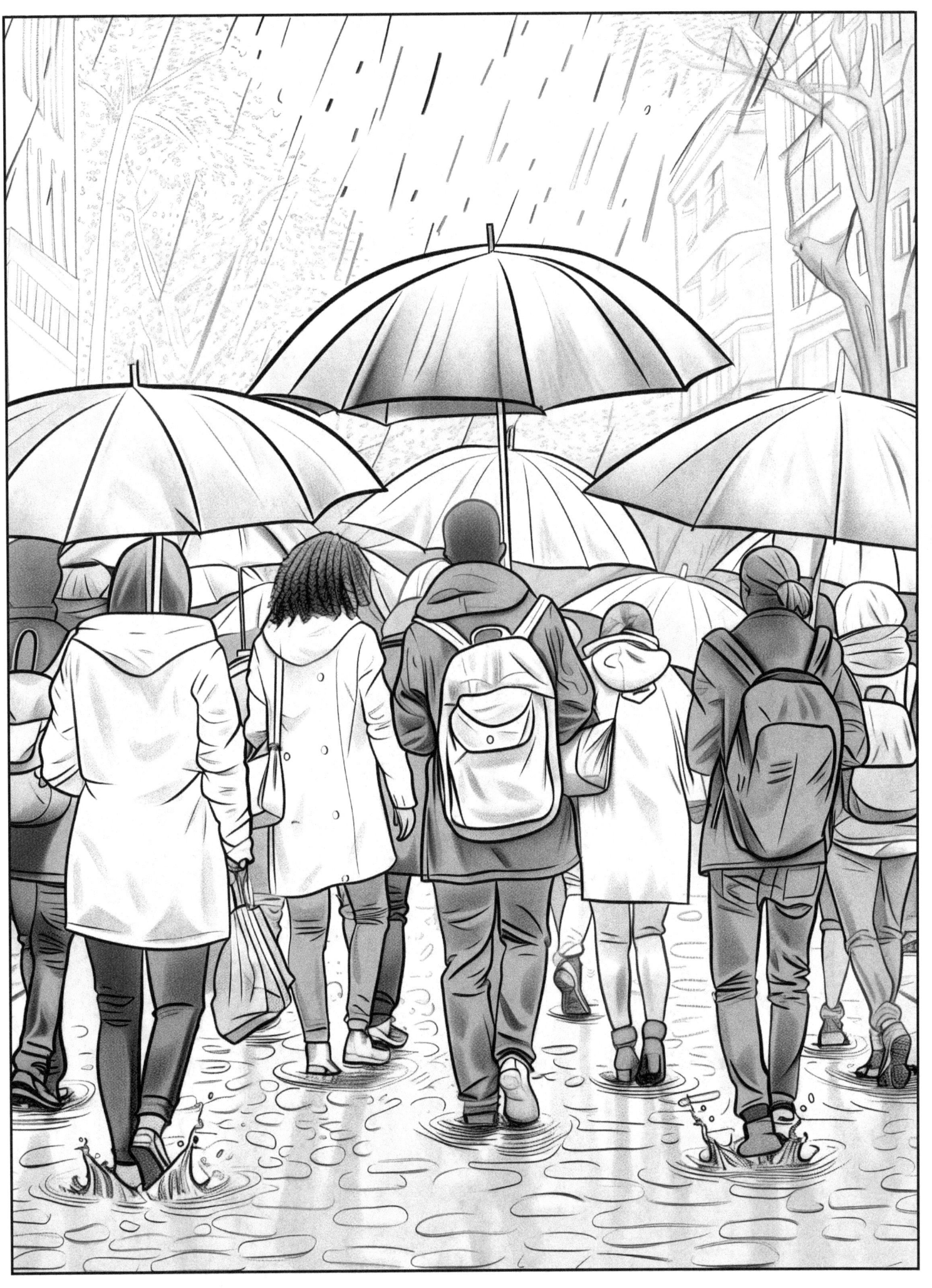

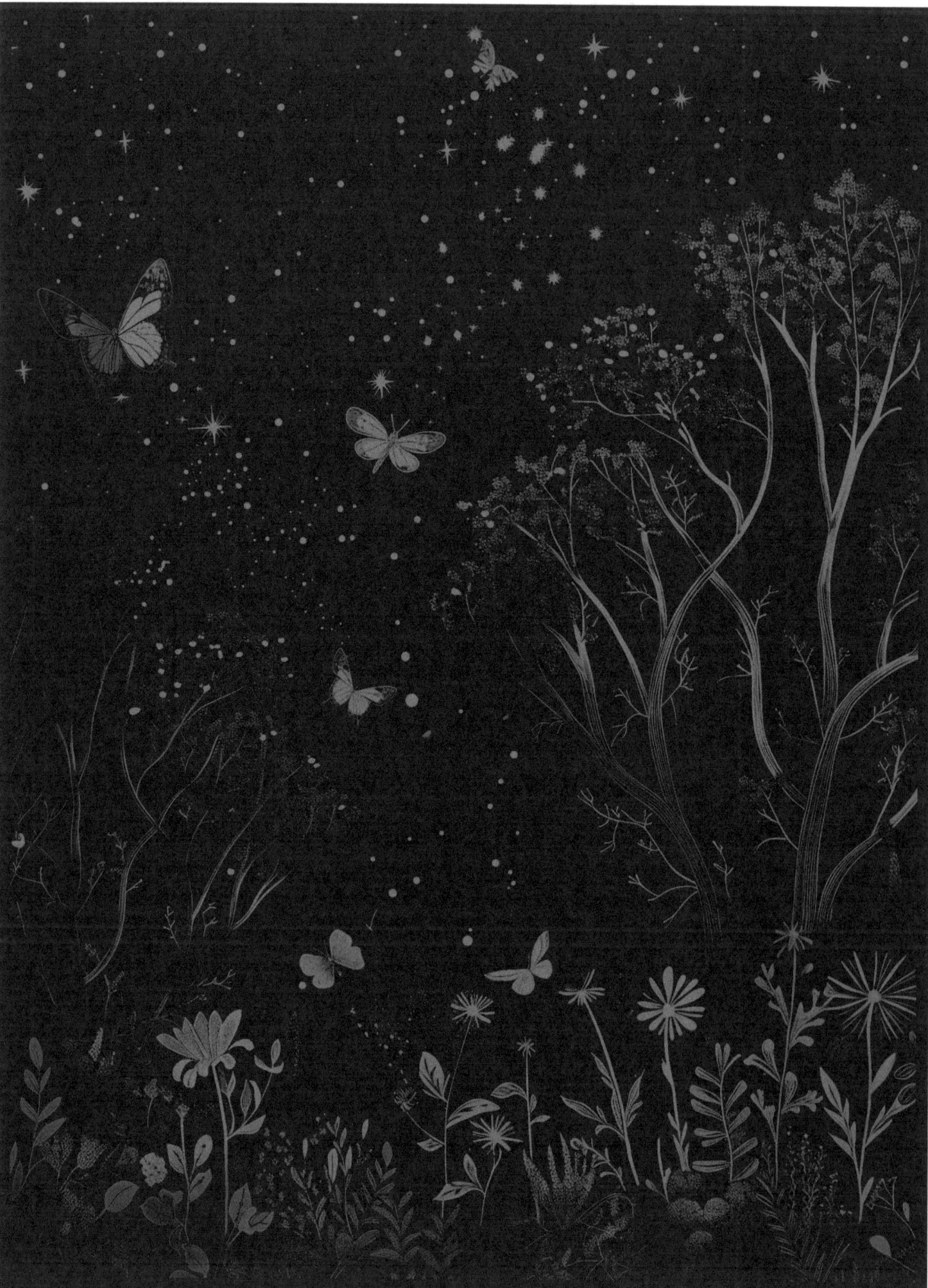

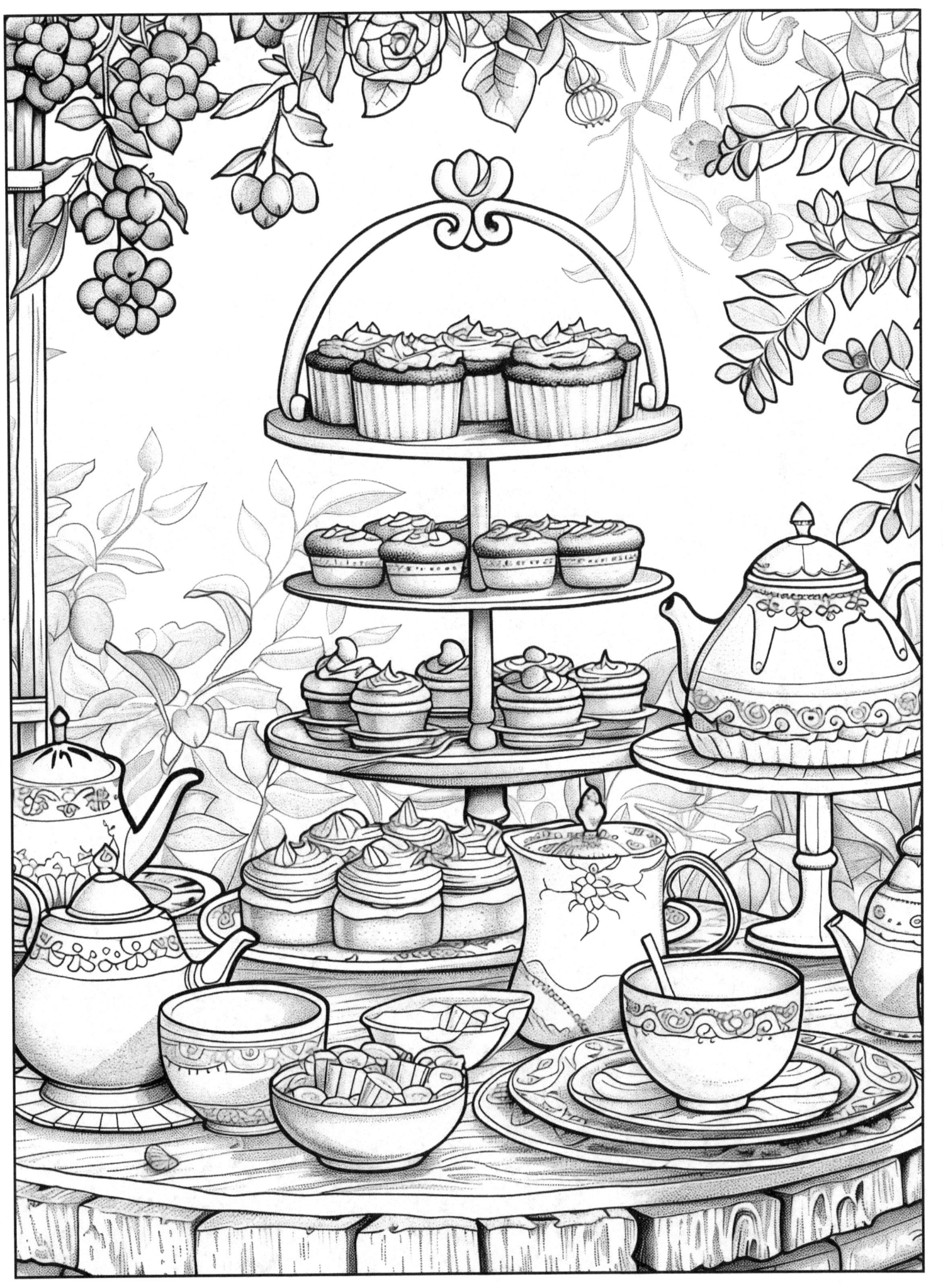

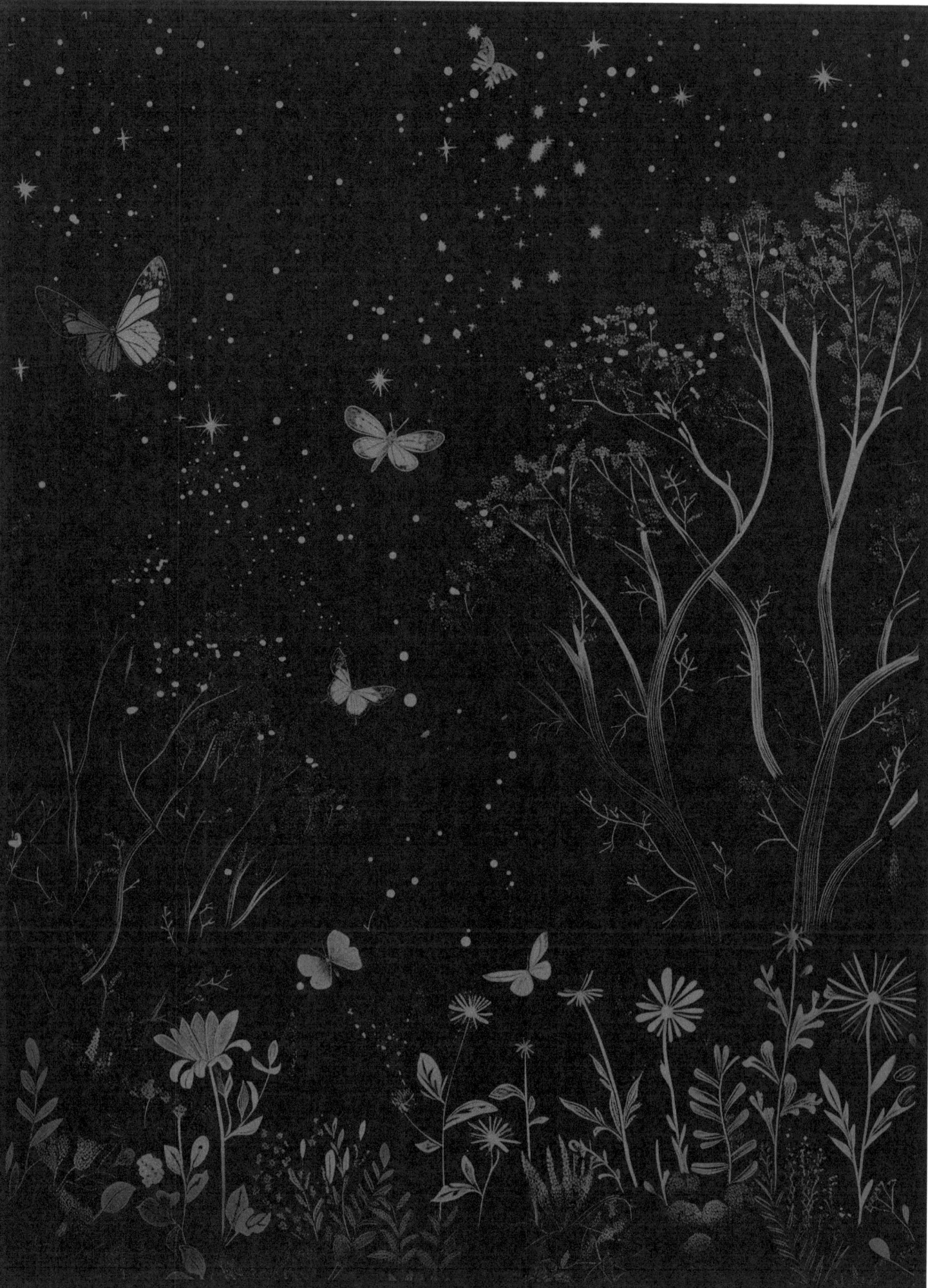

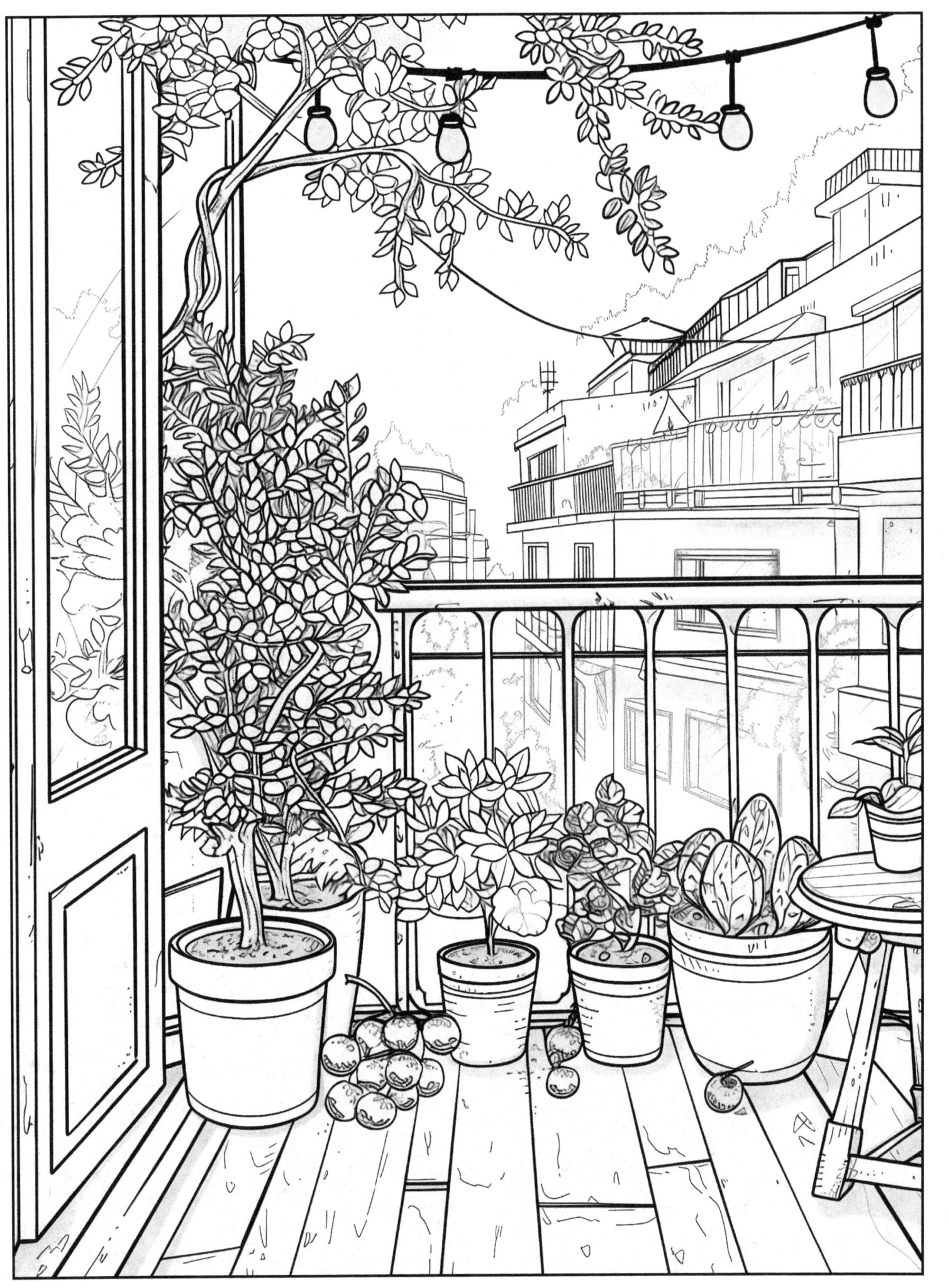

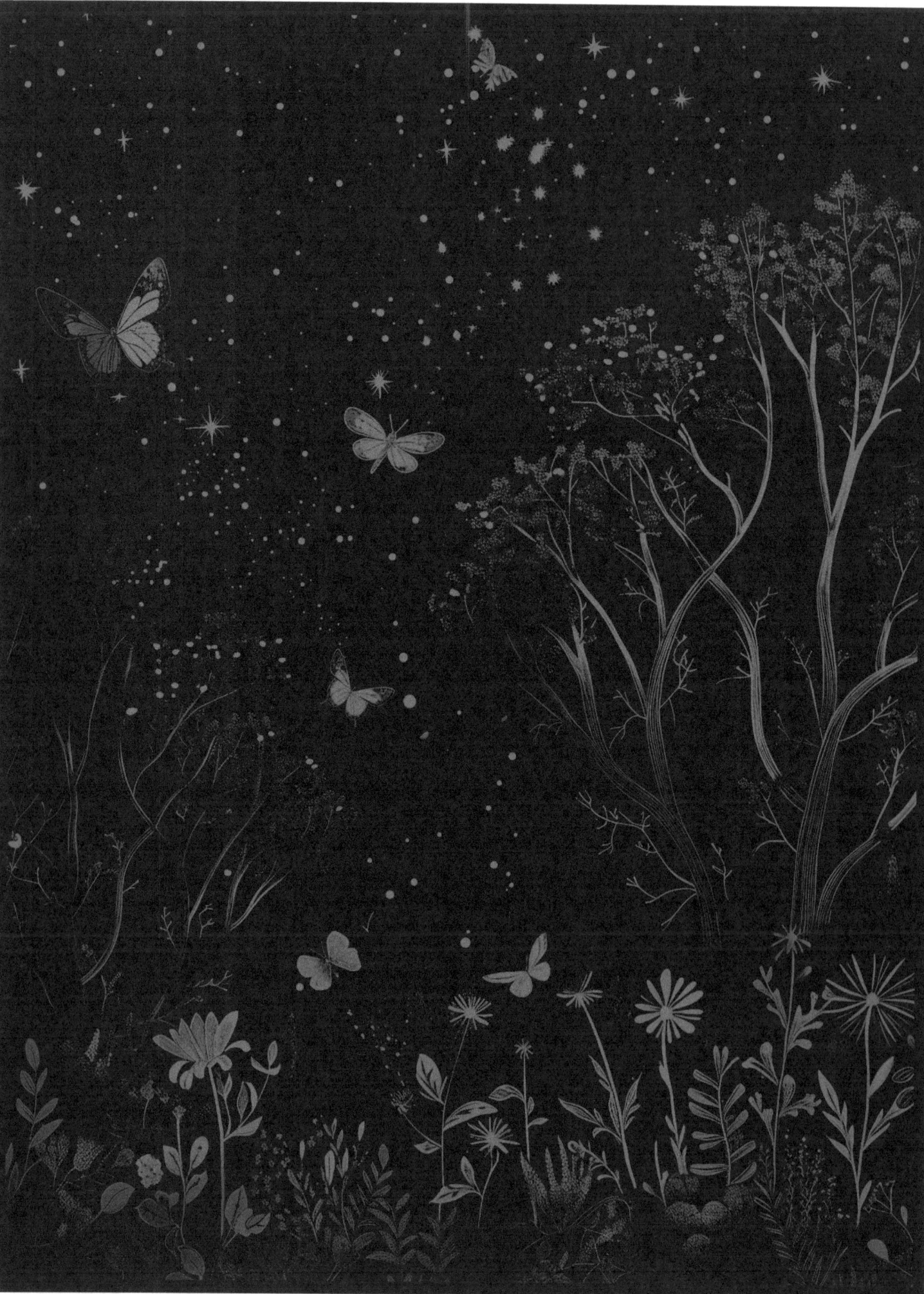

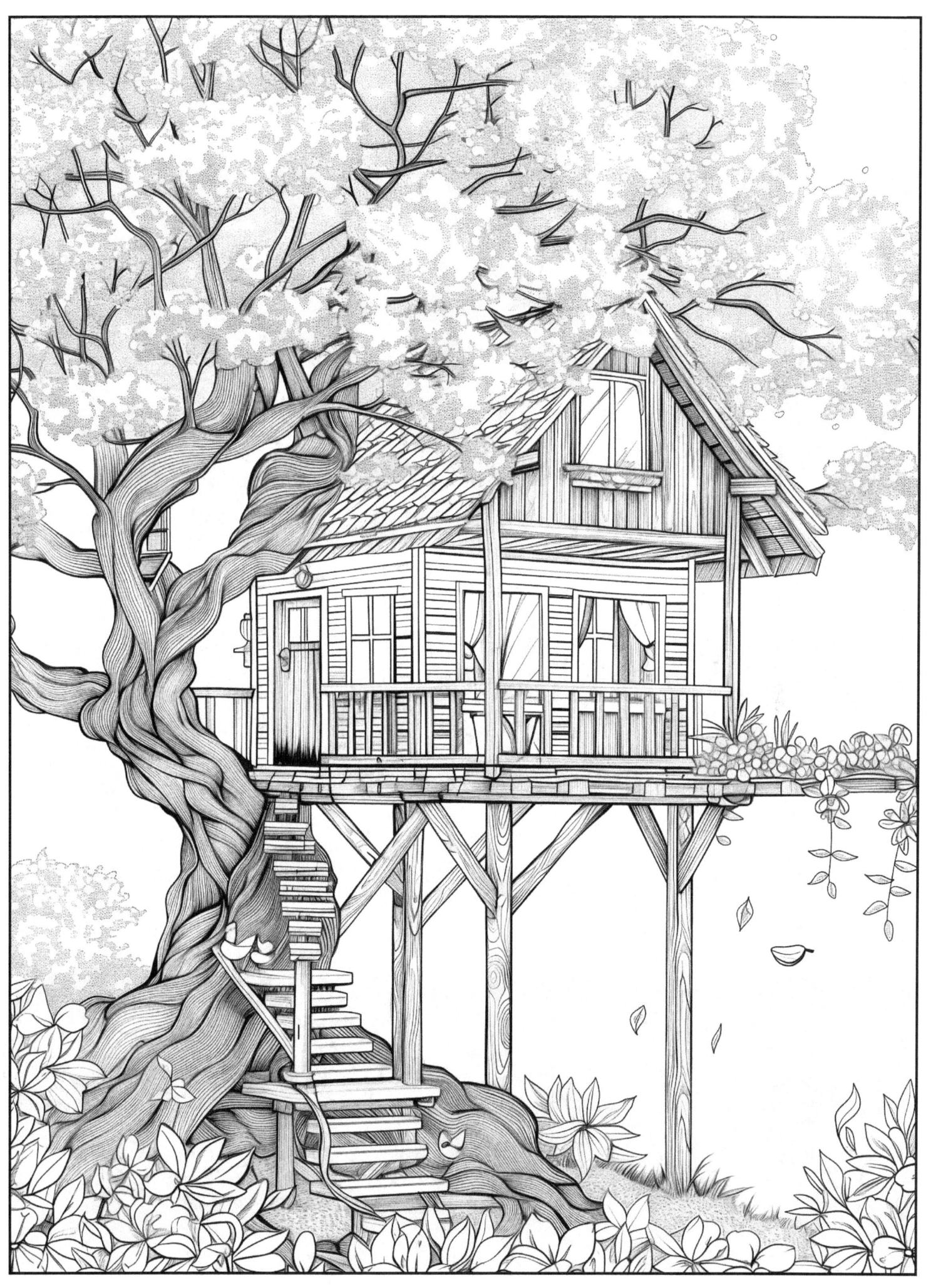

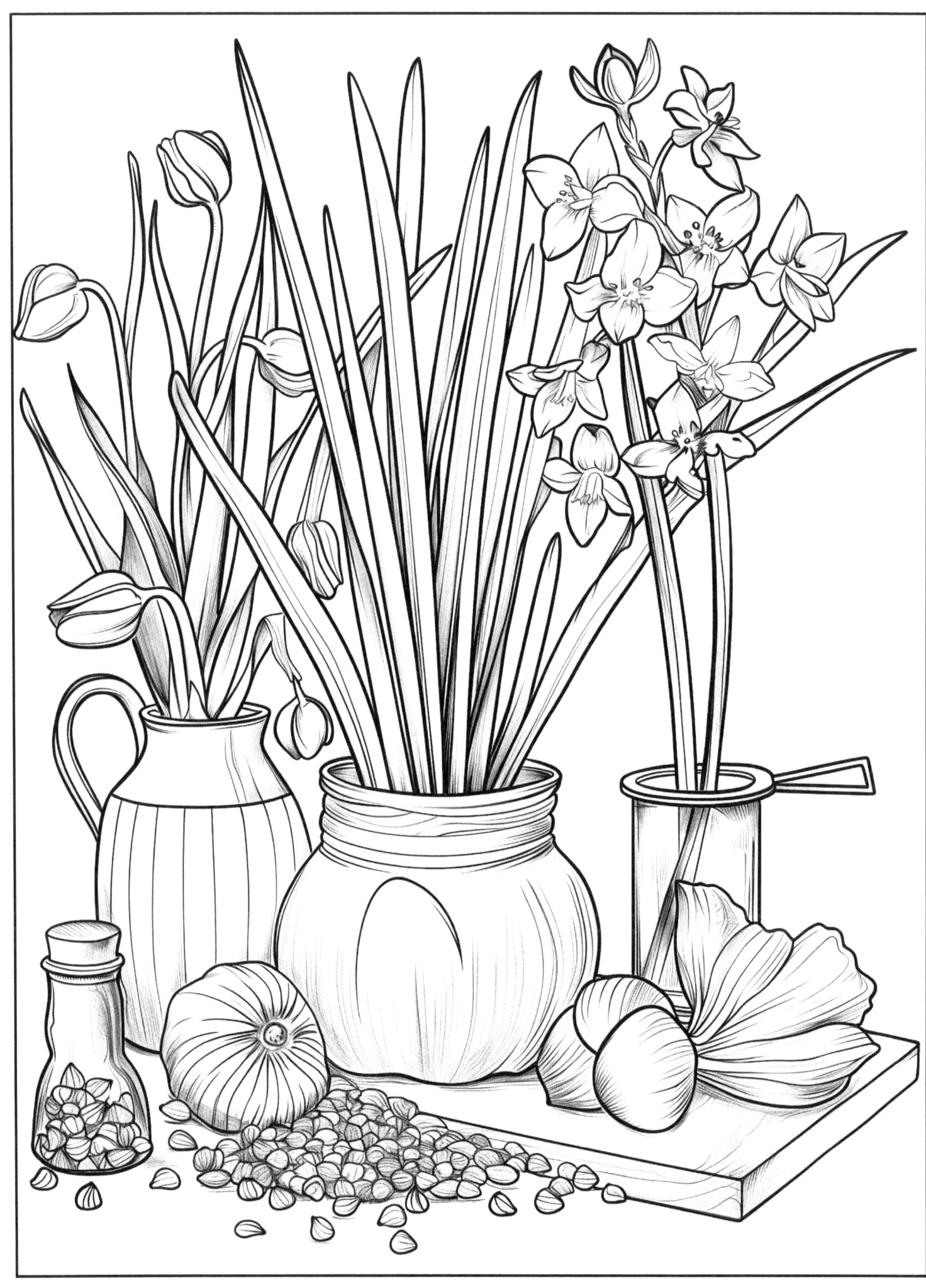

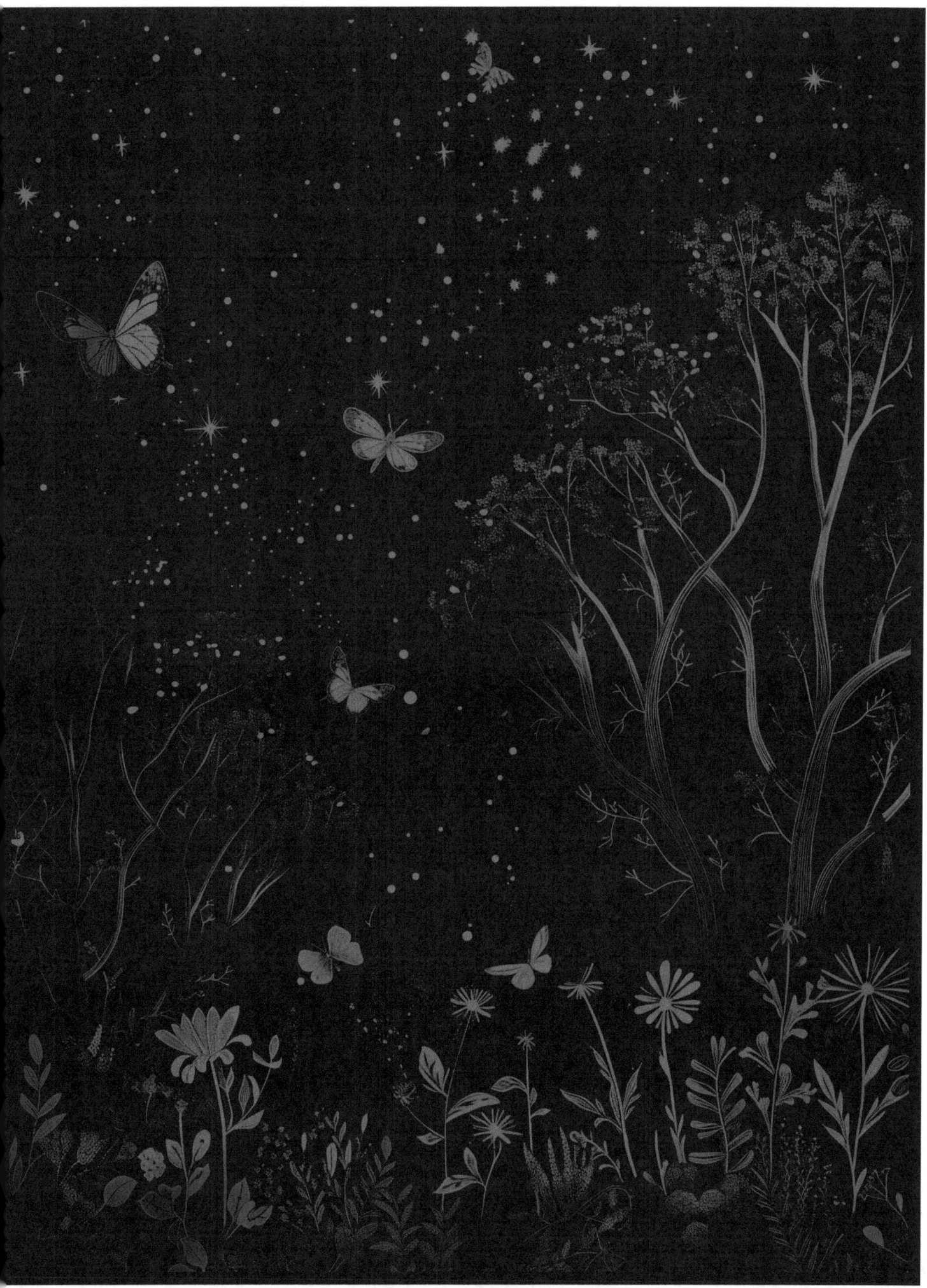

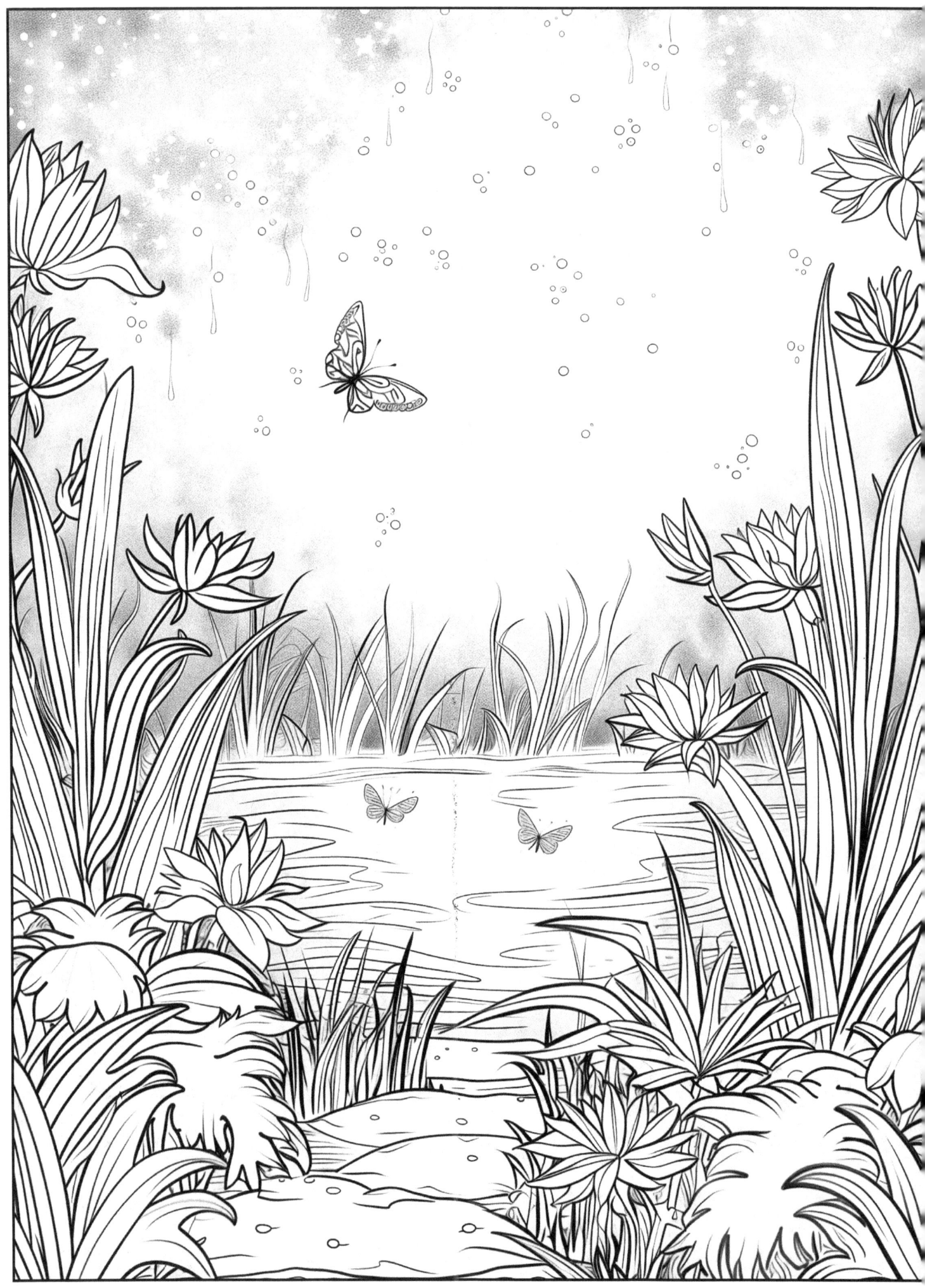

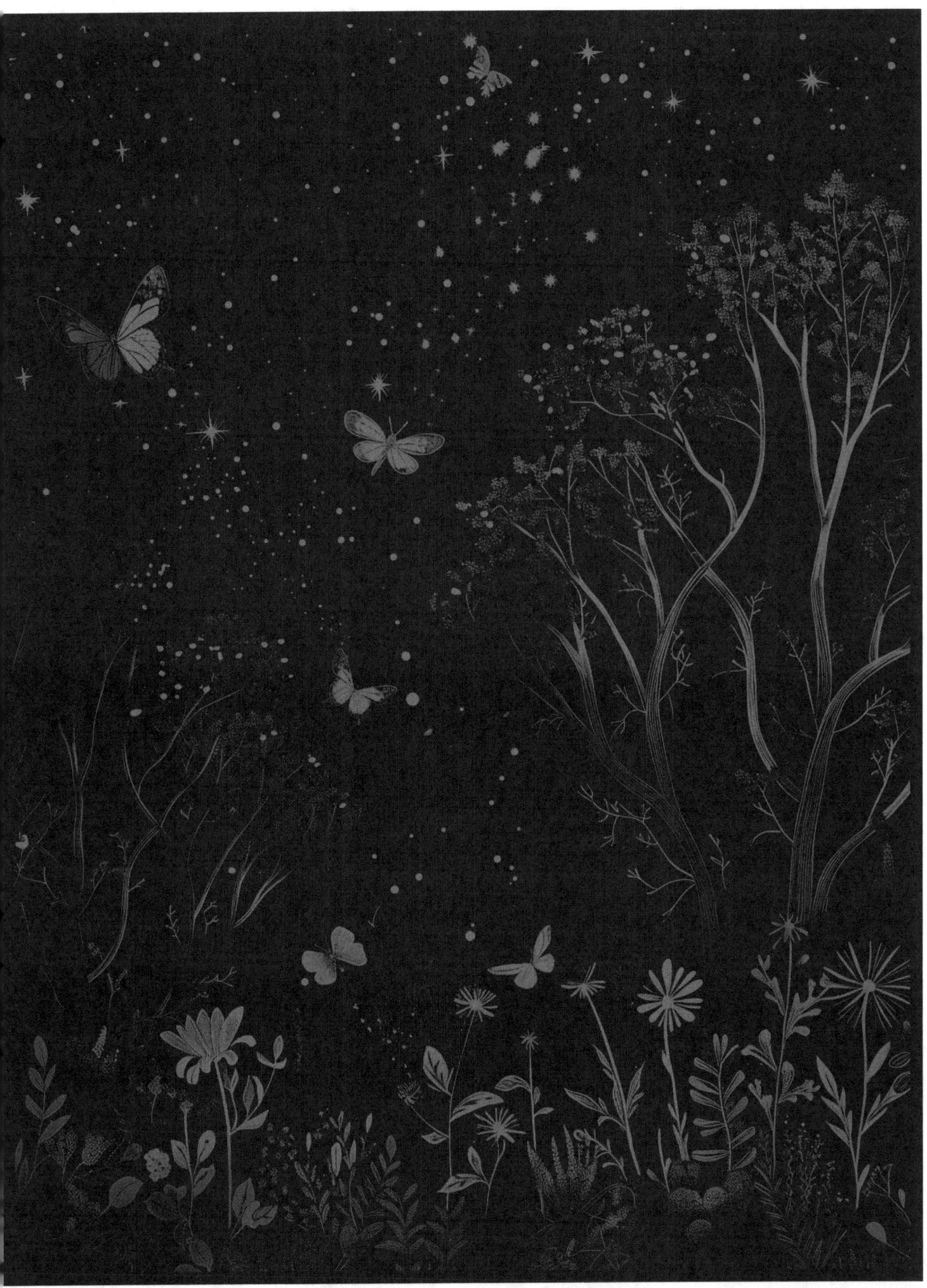

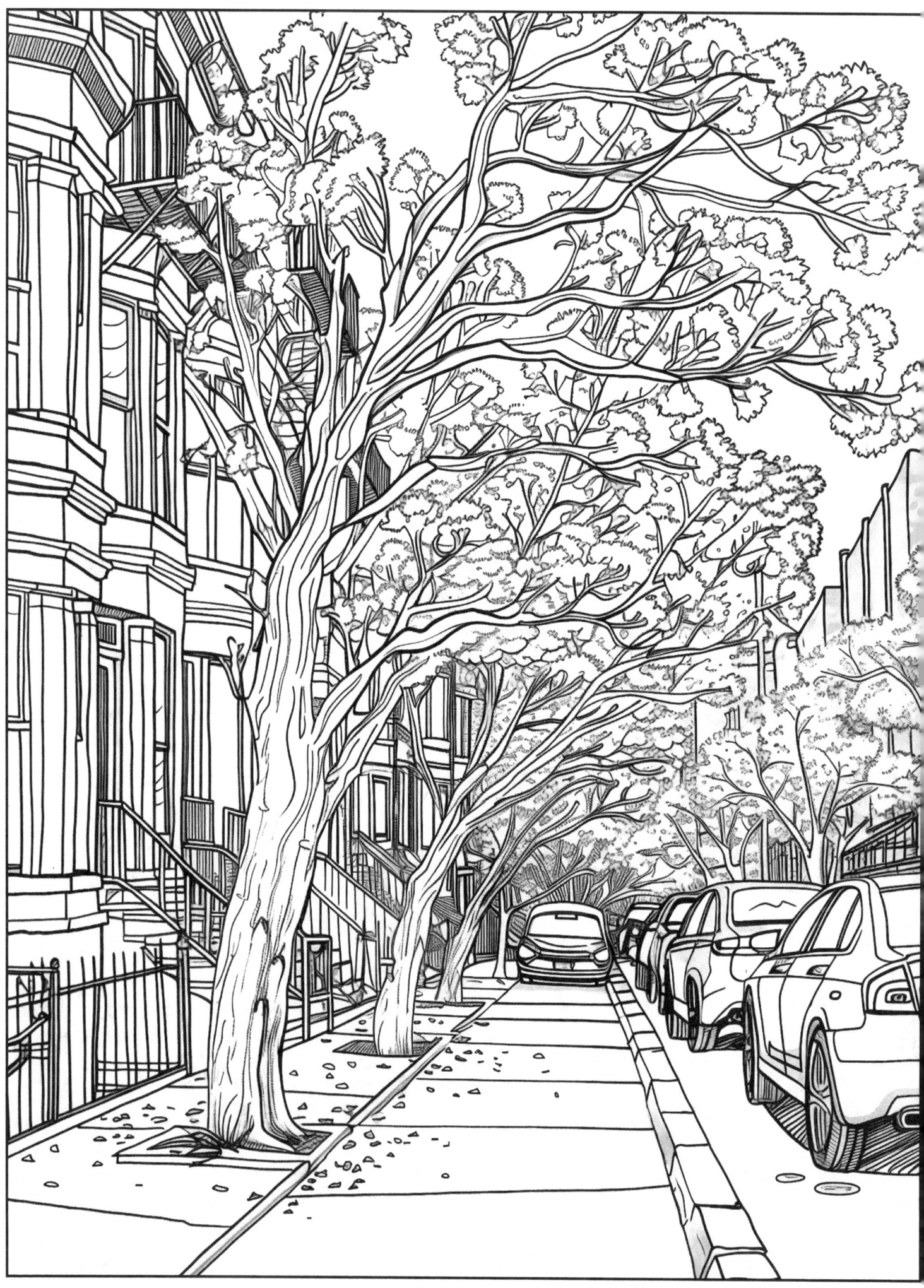

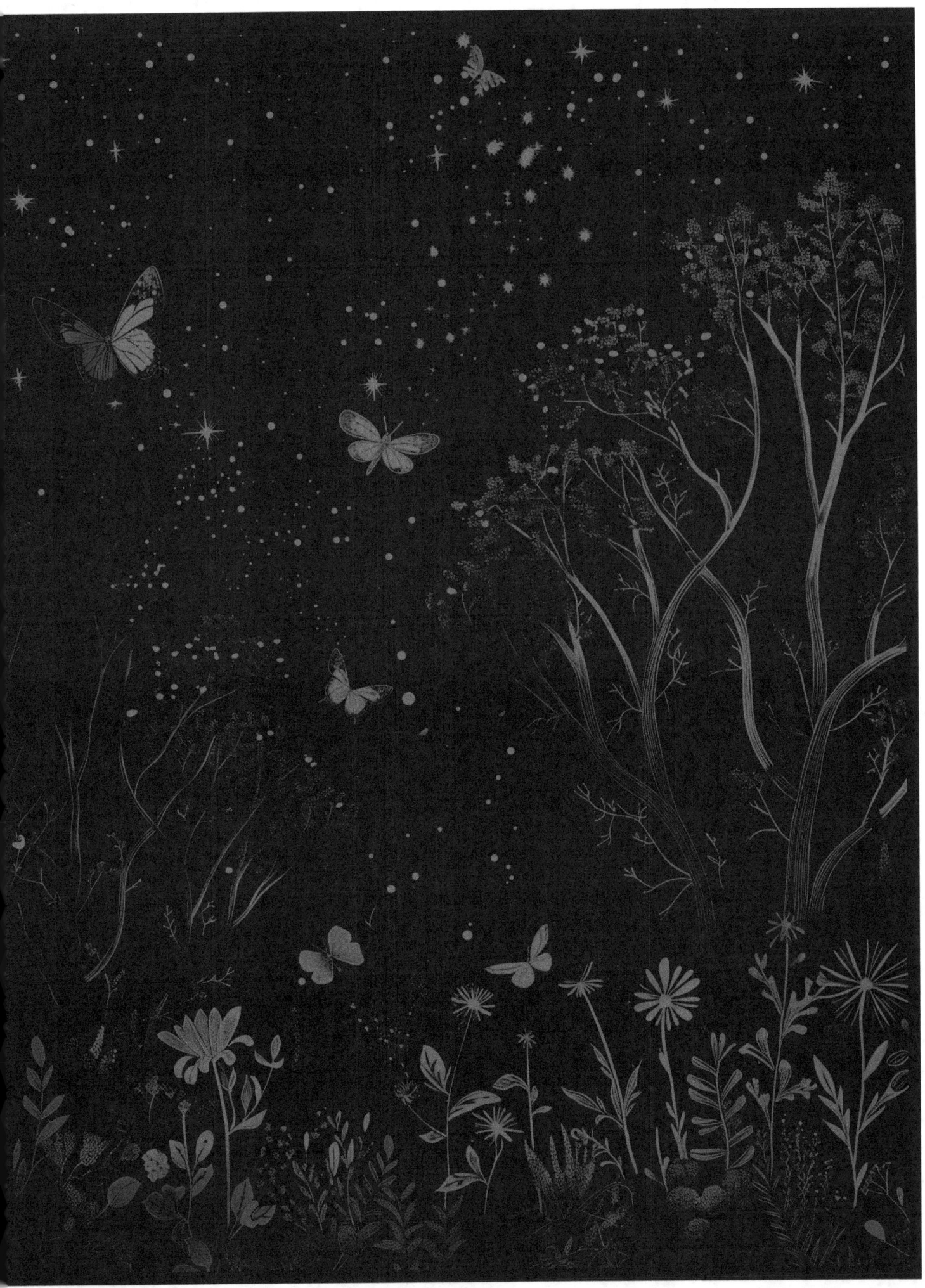

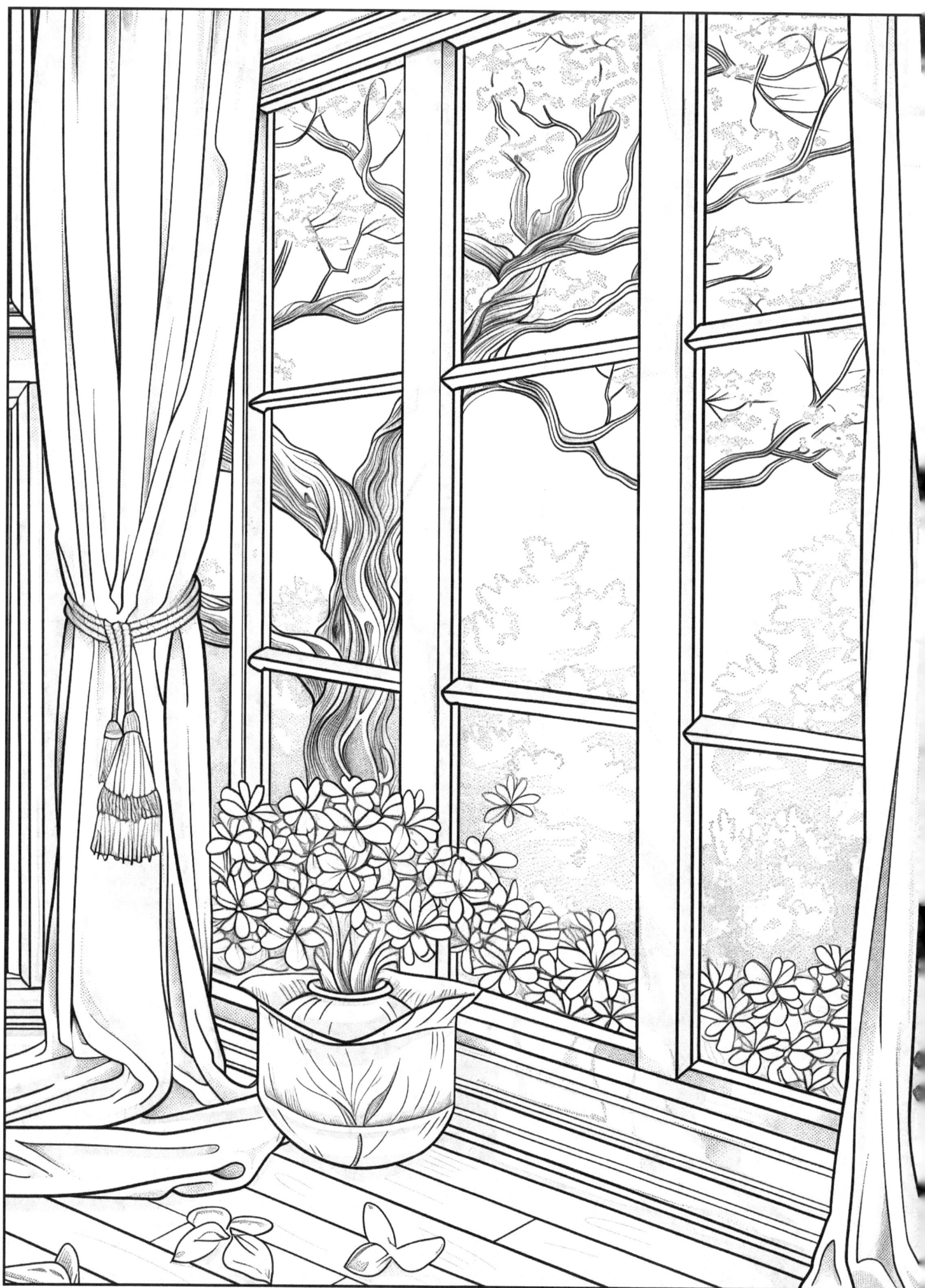

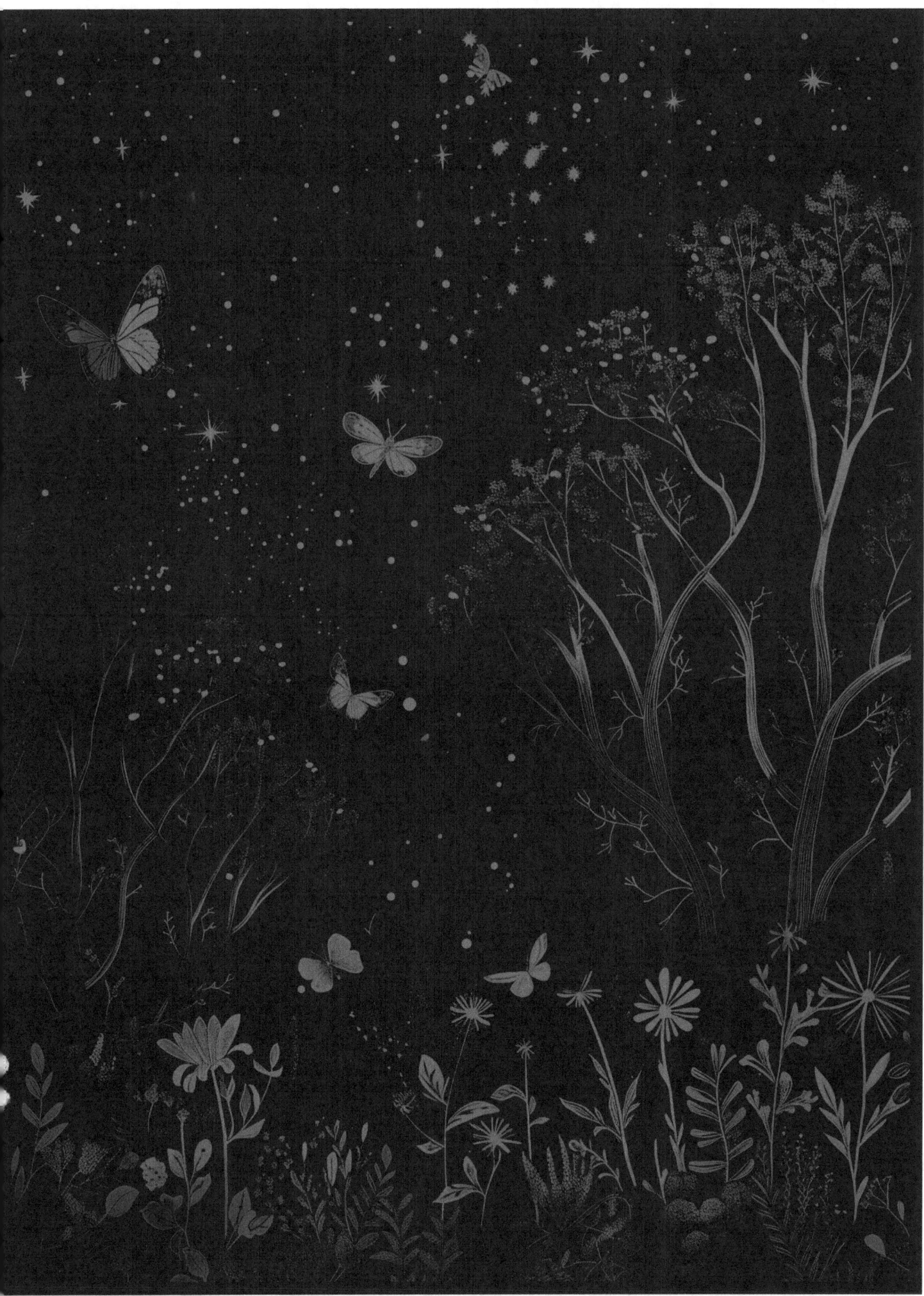

www.ingramcontent.com/pod-product-compliance
Lightning Source LLC
Chambersburg PA
CBHW062221220526
45471CB00009B/3293